THE FACES OF FRIENDSHIP

ALSO BY ISABEL ANDERS

Awaiting the Child

An Advent Journal

The
Faces
of
Friendship

Isabel Anders

COWLEY PUBLICATIONS

Cambridge ✦ *Boston*
Massachusetts

Published in the United States of America by Cowley Publications, a division of the Society of St. John the Evangelist. No portion of this book may be reproduced, stored in or introduced into a retrieval system, or transmitted, in any form or by any means—including photocopying—without the prior written permission of Cowley Publications, except in the case of brief quotations embodied in critical articles and reviews.

International Standard Book Number: 1-56101-053-7
Library of Congress Number: 91-34262

Library of Congress Cataloging-in-Publication Data
Anders, Isabel, 1946 -
    The faces of friendship / Isabel Anders.
      p. cm.
    ISBN 1-56101-053-7 (alk. paper)
    1. Friendship—Religious aspects—Christianity. I. Title.
BV4647.F7A53 1992
241'.676—dc20   91-34262

This book is printed on acid-free paper and was produced in the United States of America.

"love is a place" is reprinted from *No Thanks* by e.e. cummings, ed. by George James Firmage, by permission of Liveright Publishing Corporation. Copyright 1935 by e.e. cummings. Copyright (c) 1968 by Marion Morehouse Cummings. Copyright (c) 1973, 1978 by the Trustees for the E.E. Cummings Trust. Copyright (c) 1973, 1978 by George James Firmage.
Excerpts from "Two Citadels" from *The Unicorn and Other Poems* by Anne Morrow Lindbergh. Copyright (c) 1956 by Anne Morrow Lindbergh. Reprinted by permission of Pantheon Books, a division of Random House, Inc.
"Keepsake" from *A Miniature Cathedral and Other Poems* by Walter Wangerin, Jr. Copyright (c) 1987 by Walter Wangerin, Jr. Reprinted by permission of Harper & Row, Publishers, Inc.

Cowley Publications
28 Temple Place
Boston, Massachusetts 02111

For my parents

Acknowledgments

W ith special thanks to my editors, Theresa M. D'Orsogna, who nurtured the idea for this book and saw it grow; and for Cynthia Shattuck, who, as always, has been a friend not only of these pages but of their author.

I am grateful also to my agent, Jane Jordan Browne, for her tireless encouragement and unfailing expertise.

Table of Contents

Preface by Robert Webber

I read *The Faces of Friendship* at a particularly vulnerable point in my life and found within its pages a solace and direction I was not expecting.

The Faces of Friendship argues that a commitment in friendship begins with a comfortable relationship with one's self. For to be at peace with one's self is in itself a gift to offer another in relationship.

Then, too, this stimulating book has moved me to recognize how a true friendship is based on unity and peace with another—that the peace dwelling in one's soul is extended beyond the inner location of the self to an outer location of another. And here in friendship this person and that person swell in the inexplicable mystery of love, unity and peace.

And then beyond the glory of this relationship between two people is a relationship with God. For to dwell in unity and peace with self and neighbor is to dwell in Christ, and through him to be in God.

What an incredible framework for friendship! For God comes to us in Jesus as friend and we with our neighbor in Jesus return to God.

Thank you! What an insight on the spirituality of friendship. God grant me just one such friend and my life will be full.

Introduction

"Most of all, let love guide your life," wrote the Apostle Paul to the Colossians. "Let the peace of heart which comes from Christ be always present in your hearts and lives, for that is your responsibility and privilege as members of his body. And always be thankful" (Col. 3:14-15).

To share in the life of Christ is to be friends of God and to be in unity with each other. It is the ideal of spiritual friendship set forth in Scripture in these words:

"Love the Lord your God with all your heart and with all your soul and with all your mind. This is the first and greatest commandment. And the second is like it. *Love your neighbor as yourself*" (Matt. 22:37-39).

To see human relationships as vitally linked with the love of God is more than a moral injunction, or a pattern for "getting along with others"—it is a doorway into the school of love. It is the threshold to something Paul calls "peace," and which is also known as *serenity*. This peace, a sense of accord and unity of will, is the milieu of friendship in the Spirit.

True friendship, the love of another as self, is surely one aspect of human life that can be a reflection of the joy of heaven. According to Aelred of Rievaulx, the twelfth-century Northumbrian monk, in his classic work, *Spiritual Friendship*, "He who dwells in friendship dwells in God, and God in him."

As Christians we affirm that God is truly with us and among us, as near as our nearest neighbor. How can we love God if we do not see him? One answer has always been, through our treatment of those others, made in his image, who surround us.

"By love I do not mean natural tenderness," wrote William Law, "which is in people according to their constitution, but I see it as a larger principle of the soul, founded in reason and spiritual understanding, which makes us kind and gentle to all our fellow creatures as creations of God."

When I first began to write these reflections on friendship in the Spirit, these thoughts were the basis of my belief in a theology of friendship that has its roots in the love of neighbor as self. I envisioned writing a celebration of the many joys that are kindled through friendship, particular instances of friend connecting with friend, in my life and others' that I have observed or read of, and of an increased appreciation of the nature of friendship: how to recognize it, foster it, keep it.

But as I write, surrounded by my growing family, other people's work, needs, and demands—all the facets of daily living that are far too much of the essence of life to be called "interruptions"—I find such theology renews my faith, and spurs me on, but that I also need practical help myself each day in *how to live* as I seek to be a friend to those around me.

In this book, I hope to achieve some balance between reflecting on the everydayness of friendship—the obstacles that tend to hide it, the acts that reveal it—and the ideals and tenets of friendship that have come down to us as guidelines. In this effort, I have reached out not only to Scripture, to poetry, and to the literature of spirituality, which helps illumine a way that has been traveled—but to my daily experience and observation of friendship in the lives of others.

It is one thing to agree to this meaning of love, of friendship, even to affirm its truth in Scripture. But it is "going back to school" to submit to its pains and demands, the unmaking of our lives that the love of others may require of us. Someone has said that to love means being willing to be inconvenienced. There are times in the lessons of friendship when we wonder whether there couldn't have been an easier way!

But God's way, love of neighbor *as self*, seems to be a process that has everything to do with our own salvation, the embracing of our humanness that is the focal point of being redeemable creatures. It is only as we are realistic about ourselves, before God, that we have anything to offer others. I find increasingly that the way I treat myself as God's child, stumbling through life day to day, has much more to do with potential love of God and neighbor than I had ever thought.

I tend to be very hard on myself, sometimes to blame myself for silly mistakes—for not knowing what I could not have known at that time, yet still holding myself responsible—something I would never do to a friend. This is not only unfair to myself, diminishing my ability to love others; it also goes against reason. For some of us the lessons in love demand another look at the self before we can go any further in our progress (see Chapter Four, "Befriending Yourself").

In true friendship, our reason and our wills as well as our feelings of love are to be engaged. We *ought* to love ourselves, as we are one of those whom God loves and seeks to draw nearer to. And when we are unable to love ourselves properly, our impossible standards cannot help but stifle a deeper love of others, or create a condescension toward their inevitable disappointment of us, that clouds friendship.

If we are angry with ourselves, that is a major barrier in itself. G. Peter Fleck writes in *The Blessings of Imperfection*: "Being angry with oneself is a barren preoccupation. It wages a losing battle with the past....We want to be perfect, we want to do and say the right things...toward everybody, parents, children, friends. Forget it. Reality just isn't structured that way. Our imperfection is God-given. We have to live with our imperfection. In humility."

If I am a fallen and imperfect creature, yet I am *loved*, of God and others, then I am more able to love those around me who are accepted and held in their own humanness. We are, paradoxically, able to love much better from the reality of our own condition than from a false perfectionism that ties us up in unreality.

What are some of the imperfections that I have encountered as barriers to true friendship?

I have learned painfully that desiring good for one's friend is hardly ever without some self-interest in the matter. We dupe ourselves to think that we can stand aside from such human feelings. We are all possessed of mixed motives, yet that does not totally prevent the good that we can and do wish to those we love.

An intense desire *not* to manipulate others according to our will may mask a subtler form of manipulation that becomes a "reverse control." By our inaction, chosen uninvolvement, we may force others to take responsibility—and risk—that should be ours, at least to share.

We never truly *see* our neighbors as they are before God. Nor do our neighbors see us in this light. Only God is judge, for to God we are both visible and loved.

We can never simply hand-pick those we would have as friends and those we would exclude. Friendship happens along the journey, if we have given our assent to God's love in us. Sometimes it is very humbling, not only to have to love these others, but also to accept ourselves as lovable in these situations.

We neglect friendship, especially with those who have been placed in our path, to our great peril, and theirs. If "our neighbor's peace is half our own peace," as someone has put it, then we will reap what we have sown in the lives of others. For in truth we share one life, and that is with Christ in God.

True friendship, this willingly acknowledged connection of our lives with God and with others, costs everything, demands all, and in this context, is the only life worth pursuing. Aelred writes: "I call them more beasts than men, who say life should be led so that they need not console anyone nor occasion distress or sorrow to anyone, who take no pleasure in the good of another nor expect their failures to distress others, seeking to love no one and be loved by none."

Scripture urges us to be tenderhearted, forgiving each other. Both heart and head are called upon in the delicate task of being wise as serpents and harmless as doves toward other people. Soft of heart and hard of head is the prescription. We should not be unmoved by need and pain in others, remembering how Jesus wept at the death of his friend Lazarus. Yet we also must engage our wills, so that love is never merely awash in a sea of emotion, but full of thought and prayer for the good of ourself and the other person.

When we are willing to any degree to let go of our primary self-interest, we are all the more able to see all of creation held together by God's love, excluding none—not even ourselves. This letting go is also for our benefit, and it can teach us of the breadth of God's love. In Jesus' teaching, such a vision extends even to love of enemies, who still bear the image of God.

There are instances too, when feeling surges forth, but reason and our wills tell us at what point a friendship or a love is inappropriate and potentially damaging to us and the other, when its deeper expression might violate some other relationship, such as threaten another's marriage vows.

Friendship, love of neighbor, is both chosen and experienced, within the full range of heart and mind. But the miracle of friendship is that it *does* happen, that love breaks through, that true love casts out fear, and that when that happens, God is very near. I have seen friendships blossom in the deserts of my life, changing the landscape, restoring peace, reflecting God's love. And I have seen what looked real and solid, a friendship to rest in, suddenly dissolve into blackness. How can we know, how can we love, and continue to trust?

If, as Aelred boldly declares, "God is friendship," then we are right to be open to friendship despite our hurts; to seek both it and God, to accept the many instances of touching and caring that teach us that we are connected to God and others.

Sometimes, amid the concerns of family life, of earning a living, the demands of raising children, of working and dwelling in a household among others, it becomes easy to forget that our life together is more than the body, what we eat and what we put on. All those needs pull at us constantly, are so pressing, so immediate. They won't wait.

Friendship, especially among family and close associates, seems almost a luxury, to be worked on and developed in moments of peace (if and when they come). Then we can finally "do something for ourselves" and others, take a look at friendship after everything else is settled, in those few moments we have for each other at the end of the day.

Yet my experience is becoming just the opposite: That elusive time of quiet and space, if and when it comes, is only part of the story of friendship. It is rather, I have discovered, *in* the fray, between impossible demands of dinner-on-the-table immediately, work deadlines, endless picking up and sorting, cleaning and caring for houses and lands, struggling together, seeking words that bear the truth, that love springs out—or burrows through, revealing itself like plants emerging through sidewalk cracks. And this is as it should be.

Friendship is here, in our life, in loving phone calls that punctuate a late evening's quiet; cards and letters that bear more than simple greetings—prayers between the lines; the hug of a little one and "I love you" whispered for no tangible reason; a loving birthday present; a dozen roses remembered for an anniversary.

There is plenty wrong in ourselves and in the world that interferes with the delicate task of friendship. And a lot of it—the discord, dissension, anger, and alienation—occurs in families and with others we are closest to. Garrison Keillor writes that "when I was twenty...I felt that a true sign of intelligence was restlessness and dissatisfaction. But somewhere along the line, I began to think that another task of intelligent people is to describe what we love."

For me, a book about friendship is describing what I love, and celebrating the fact that it *can* exist—persist—despite our own blindness and failures, neglect and miscalculations. It is even more remarkable that friendship can grow and spread, even in this imperfect, helter-skelter world in which it sometimes seems that everyone is out for his own benefit, merely to survive. Friendship affirms that more than survival is possible: peace and unity are to be a way of life, a life with and for others which can only be lived one day at a time. This, for me, is the abundant life of which Christ spoke.

And as I write, I seek to teach myself what being a friend has meant and can yet mean in the circumstances of my life. True friendship occurs in those moments of grace when we become caught up in another's triumph, and gain for oneself drops away. Rather, we can step aside to let others have their moment, to be framed with love and care, because they are so unmistakably children of God who have mysteriously appeared in our path.

Who is my neighbor? What is a friend? And how can I be one in *this life* and among *these* people? I hope to address some of the characteristics of Christian friendship, as well as ways in which we inevitably fail each other; the need to focus beyond ourselves and forego the need to try to control others. It is a lifelong task to view friendship and all relations in the light of the life for which we were created—here and hereafter.

Friendship means laughter, sometimes so hard to find in the effort and stress of "making things work." Thus I pray, while seeking to examine the seriousness of friendship, to also have that veil of "oughtness" lifted time and again, to draw attention to the playfulness that also can be part of the dance of friends through stages and transitions in life.

For some of these wonderful examples of unbridled joy I look to my own children, who are my teachers as well as fellow learners in the school of love. For they have not yet forgotten how to play, to learn through a continual search for and openness to delight. I marvel at the way they continue to discover on a basic level all the various types of lessons, challenges, and relationships that they will encounter and reprise as adults.

"Now I don't have a friend," my daughter Sarah used to lament, at age three, when she was temporarily left alone in a room. In her protected world of love and loving, care and guidance, she has learned to rely instinctively on someone being there—with her, beside her, and for her.

I have my own, growing adult understanding of friendship— how seeds are planted and reaped in their time; some relationships which grow to a healthy height, and others that are clipped off in mid-growth—friendships flourishing, luxuriant as grass, others dormant but not dead.

The faces of friendship are ever changing, adding, and, sadly, being lost, as well. But it is hard to improve on Sarah's idea of a friend as simply *someone who is there for you*.

Perhaps a friend is not always in close proximity, as Sarah will learn, when her understanding of what a friend *is* widens in its application. A friend may seem to be—or actually be—silent and even absent in one's world for a while, for deliberate or unintentional reasons. But if that person was truly a friend from the start, "the garden will tell," as a true friend of mine once wrote.

A friend is one whose essential beingness, whose presence in the world, has touched ours at some point. And from such points of touching we measure our time, our very lives before and after.

My wish for Sarah, as she grows in her experiences and understanding of friendship, is that she will increasingly find joy in the reality of the others she touches. I pray that, without losing her instinctive wisdom, she will add to it the pleasures of heart and mind, and learn from going through the turns and stops of the engagement with others we call friendship.

Samuel Johnson has called friendship "one of the greatest comforts of this weary pilgrimage," and indeed it is the presence of others that makes our journey more bearable. Friendship offers us a unique opportunity to cherish the world in all its variety of human expression, its joys and challenges.

Flannery O'Connor has said, "You have to cherish the world at the same time you struggle to endure it." By the light of each other's presence mirrored on the faces of those around us, and in mutual giving, we can sometimes endure.

As I step over broken crayons, run out in a thunderstorm on an errand of love, or stop for seemingly the hundredth time on one page of an article I'm trying to read, to break up a fight, it's hard to look beyond the moment, to believe in abundance just around the corner, a life together that friendship redeems and makes meaning of for eternity. Often I am too drained to see beyond my own survival in the moment, and peace and serenity—not to mention unity of will—seem unattainable. But friendship says in all our acts of love toward others, small and particular though they may be, the bonds of life are strengthened and secured; that others are there as part of that Heavenly City that overlaps heaven and earth; that their presence with, beside, and for us is part of salvation itself.

C. S. Lewis wrote that "next to the Blessed Sacrament itself, our neighbour is the holiest object presented to our senses." He reminds us that "you have never talked to a mere mortal...it is immortals whom we joke with, work with, marry, snub, and exploit...."

Clearly, our actions toward others are of great significance to God, who put such behavior second in the Great Commandment: "Thou shalt love the Lord thy God with all thy heart....*And...thy neighbor as thyself.* On these two commandments hang all the law and the prophets" (Matt. 22:37-40).

To see this great command juxtaposed with ordinary life is to catch a glimpse of friendship in the Spirit. It's impossible to live up to it, but precarious not to ask for the grace to try.

In these pages we will look at some simple ways in which friendship can be recognized for what it truly is, encouraged, built upon, and appreciated. Friendship can never be forced, or, like a developing plant, it will collapse. But it can be watered and fed and then it may grow, for as long as two wills agree to it and persist in its nurture.

I will write in these pages my reflections of friendship as it has occurred to me and others, glimpses of times when friendship seemed possible and when it has faltered, sometimes in heartbreaking ways. To look at one's own life among others, as it is being lived, is risky and costly. Yet the more we can both reflect, learn and grow, and reach out to others, where they are— see, touch, and embrace all that life among others has to offer us—the more we will see God's kingdom come, here and now.

Novelist Frederick Buechner in his memoir *Now and Then*, writes of a time when he found the courage to begin to write of his own life in all its everydayness, realizing that it could open up into "extraordinary vistas." His advice to others who would share the mystery of God present in their lives—"taking your children to school and kissing your wife good-bye. Eating lunch with a friend"—is "Listen to your life. See it for the fathomless mystery that it is. In the boredom and pain of it no less than in the excitement and gladness: touch, taste, smell your way to the holy and hidden heart of it because in the last analysis all moments are key moments, and life itself is grace."

These moments of grace are what Christian friendship is all about. I begin with a look at friendship with God, and with Christ, the starting point for any friendship in the Spirit. I also look at close relationships, at some significant moments with, among, and sometimes through the eyes of those nearest to me. This means traveling back in time to where our first idea of being-with-others occurs, in the family. To return with new eyes, to look at those experiences and their lessons, is to find that the locale of friendship has always been the region of the heart, with no closer point to God available than our first encounters with human love.

Here are faces of friendship that have blessed and troubled, hurt and challenged—not unlike the many faces all of us encounter daily. If, as Dostoevsky has said, "to love someone means to see him as God intended him," I pray for eyes to see the faces that I love only more clearly in the days and years to come.

CHAPTER ONE

To Be a Friend of God

I t is in and through Christ, his work on the cross, his love extended to us from the Father, that we are called to be friends with God. In his great discourse on friendship, Aelred of Rievaulx wrote, "For what more sublime can be said of friendship, what more true, what more profitable, than that it ought to, and is proved to, begin in Christ, continue in Christ, and be perfected in Christ?"

This is the point at which we begin, as have so many Christian writers as they attempt to tell their own stories. Are not the lives of the saints, ancient and modern, stories of friendship? They tell of God's particular dealings with one soul, the intimacy and the acts that have proceeded from that very relationship.

Friendship with God, in Christ, is a pervasive occupation of the Christian, and all other relationships and activities are somehow to be found in the light of that commitment. Brother Lawrence urges us to "practice the presence of God" this way:

"Think often on God, by day, by night, in your business, and even in your diversions. He is always near you and with you; leave Him not alone. You would think it rude to leave a friend alone who came to visit you; why, then, must God be neglected?...Adore Him continually, live and die with Him; this is the glorious employment of a Christian; in a word, this is our profession; if we do not know it we must learn it."

Christians, according to their temperament and experience, have had greatly differing ideas of the texture of this friendship with God. One popular hymnwriter set the tone for friendship in his word-picture of one walking in the Garden with Christ alone, with "dew on the roses"—an intimate fellowship of friends. Christ, in this picture is comforting, his voice gentle and caring, his words as tender as that of a lover, walking and talking with us as though we were the only person in the universe.

Such a view could so easily be sentimentalized and even dismissed by a cynical eye. But it describes the flavor of one experience of friendship some have had in their relationship with Christ. It seems a reflection of the kind of occasional walk one of Jesus' disciples might have had with him, which gave them strength for the trials ahead.

Other saints have had quite contrasting experiences of the friendship of God. Some have even dared to record the honest doubts and silences that made them question God's presence with and for them in the moment. They remind us that our humanity is always part of the picture, that the horizontal crossbar of our lives cuts across and defines, crosslike, our relationship with God.

I think of that famous story that is often told of St. Teresa, in the throes of difficult travel, fallen in the mud with her mule, dejected and frustrated, perhaps holding her fist to the sky. She retorts, "God, if this is the way you treat your friends, it is no wonder you have so few of them!" Surely this is not what we had in mind when we turned to God and reached out for the help and assurance that we were not alone in this ravaging world.

We have looked to God for friendship, for comfort and help in our circumstances. Thus in moments of distress we feel acutely God's silence, a seeming absence, precisely because we have expected something else. Yet all of Scripture testifies that even this is part of Christ's promise that "I am with you always," a truth that can only be apprehended by faith. In Psalm 105 we are commanded to "search for the Lord and his strength; continually seek his face."

Writer Robert Farrar Capon in his book *The Third Peacock*, sheds interesting light on two aspects of friendship, as it relates to God and to others:

"When we say that a friend 'helped' us, two meanings are possible. In the case where our need was a Band-Aid, a gallon of gas or a push on a cold morning, we have in mind mechanical help, help for times when help was at least possible. But when nothing can be helped"—when there is no easy answer—"when the dead are irretrievably dead and the beloved lost for good," it is *presence* that matters, not mechanical help. "The only way [God's help] makes any sense is when it's seen as personal:

When we are helpless, there he is. Jesus is blithely paradoxical—or inconsistent, if you like....His chief concern is to *be himself for you*. And since he is God, that is no small item."

Friendship with God, as we even find the boldness to speak of it, is a matter of *being*, and of being ourselves with God, as God is God with us.

Jesus has taught us through his own story, in his life on earth, some of the fullness and breadth of what being with a friend entails and demands—that it consists in supping and rejoicing and sharing daily life, but that it also includes suffering. Friendship with Christ, identification with God in this personal way, means that each of our individual lives will in some manner follow the way of the cross. We see this pattern of friendship with God in the lives of all the saints, as inexorable as the very shape of our bodies, molded in the cross-form of the Christ who was broken for us.

Frederick Buechner wrote in *The Magnificent Defeat*, "What we need to know, of course, is not just that God exists, not just that beyond the steely brightness of the stars there is a cosmic intelligence of some kind that keeps the whole show going, but that there is a God right here in the thick of our day-to-day lives who may not be writing messages about deity in the stars, but who in one way or another is trying to get messages through our blindness as we move around down here knee-deep in the fragrant muck and misery and marvel of the world."

This is friendship as we can understand it, for in his immanence, his presence with and among us, God's life touches our own. To talk of such friendship with God is also to talk of ourselves, our journey, the times in particular when that message of friendship with God has "gotten through," banged us on the head or whispered to us in the midst of a prayer. It may have come to us in the voice of a friend beside us, in tragedy or despair, in the written word, in retrospect, in choices and in pleasures along the way.

It is clear that friendship with God and each other partakes in all the "muck and misery and marvel"—as St. Teresa found—and is never divorced from what is human about us, especially what Christ showed us about being human in his life on earth.

To look at it another way, perhaps to say that one is a "friend of God" or a "friend of Jesus" is almost to have it backwards, or to begin at the wrong starting point. It may seem presumptuous, a case of taking oneself too seriously in assuming we have something to offer God, who already has all things in hand, or that we could possibly add anything to the Godhead by offering our friendship. But extending our friendship and our commitment is surely and simply the response that God invites us to make.

Jesus told his disciples, in the context of a message both comforting and warning them of trials to come, "I no longer call you servants, because a servant does not know his master's business. Instead, I have called you friends..." (John 15:15).

What a word of affirmation from One they had come to know, to live and work with day to day, observing all his conduct—whose "business" with the Father (v. 15b) was at least somewhat clearer to them at this point. This relationship was not to be all quiet walks of serene fellowship, shared meals and confidences—the work of healing and preaching and miracles. The invitation of connection with God the Father which Jesus was to extend to his disciples would include also the dusty road to the cross, the shame and misunderstanding, the loneliness, the doubts—and the fear that God himself had forsaken them, as he at the end seemed to have deserted his own Son.

What would it entail to stand with, by, and for Jesus on the road that lay ahead of him? As we know from Scripture and tradition, it was to mean that the disciples would do great deeds in the name of their Friend, or as some have said, "turn the world upside down" in the name of Christianity. But it would also mean that the world would "hate" them for their efforts, as it had hated Christ (15:18). What a legacy for a friendship! Clearly it is not a mantle to be taken on lightly. We must know something more of the nature of this friendship in order to walk in it, prepared for the reality.

As Capon puts it, God "doesn't start your stalled car for you; he comes and dies with you in the snowbank. You can object that he should have made a world in which cars don't stall; but you can't complain he doesn't stick by his customers."

It may seem shocking and even a bit flip to speak of friendship with God in such ways, but it is an important antidote to the sentimentality of so many simplistic concepts of God being our "friend," ideas that tend to make *us* seem special, or unduly immune from the ordeals that others may face. The consuming demands of friendship with God, what Brother Lawrence called "our profession," our "glorious employment," go along with the more serene aspects of that sense we sometimes have of walking hand in hand, in peace and safety, with our Lord. It is a great paradox. We are never more human than when we are both fully involved and invested in our own life with its particular challenges and demands, joys and griefs, and when we are simultaneously holding God's hand through it all.

Once when I was going through a very difficult time, struggling to accept the sudden loss of someone dear to me, I went to my pastor in a very broken spirit, seeking assurance. I was desperate for real and tangible evidence that God was in this, that God was a strong and unyielding presence, a loving Father, and Christ still my friend—that I had not been utterly forsaken. Sensing the focus of my pain, he handed me a Bible open to John 15, a very familiar passage—and I read again, as though for the first time:

"I am the vine, you are the branches....Apart from me you can do nothing....Greater love has no one than this, that he lay down his life for his friends. You are my friends if you do what I command....You did not choose me, but I chose you." Not only my desire to *be* in the present moment, the will to go on in my grief, but my entire sense of choice and freedom had been dangerously impaired. These words from John's gospel of God's having acted and chosen *me* as a friend, standing with me even in the muck and cold of this situation, gave exactly the reassurance I needed.

Even in this experience, with a wise pastoral guide, within the community of other believers, and in a place of peace, I cannot say that all pain fell away or that I was lifted immediately from my grief. But rather, being able to take God's hand again, know Christ's love, was a way to take steps out of the mire and head again toward solid ground.

Friendship with God is based on this fact: that it is God who extends the friendship, in Christ, and we accept this on faith. Friendship with God is a work of the Spirit, a connection with the life of God that is granted to us, that comes down to us as life flows from the branch to the vines. We could no more change that fact than leaves could exist in the dirt on their own, without a source of life and nourishment.

And how are vines to experience this vital connection? To be exactly what they are, to adhere, to continue to accept friendship with God in Christ, as it is offered. And we are called, as I was in my distress, to *be*, to affirm the connection, to keep on living in the relationship that already existed, to find a way to flourish and to bear fruit even in the face of loss. It is always a matter of faith, of trust, to acknowledge that God is indeed there, that the shape of the cross fits our circumstances today, a reminder that Christ is ever-present, the friend who sticks closer than a brother.

It is not easy for me to write of friendship, so close and personal a relationship, with God. As a believer, I have always been "afflicted with transcendence," that opposite side of the paradox of God's nearness. For Christian orthodoxy affirms that God is both with and among us—and totally Other: that God is immanent in our world, as well as utterly transcendent.

The idea and fact of God's transcendence has, from earliest recollections, been both evident and attractive to me. I have always been in awe of the glory of creation, cherished a love of beauty and poetry, and longed for increased vision of the wholeness of things. This belief that unity exists, and that we can somehow find a place of harmony for ourselves in the context of the whole, is the core of the mystic's view.

One strikingly beautiful expression of this vision is found in Dom Bede Griffith's autobiographical book *The Golden String*. In it he quotes Blake's famous lines,

> I give you the end of a golden string;
>   Only wind it into a ball,
> It will lead you in at heaven's gate,
>   Built in Jerusalem's wall.

Griffith writes of an experience of overwhelming beauty in the joy of creation in which, on one occasion, he felt as "if I had been brought suddenly among the trees of the Garden of Paradise and heard a choir of angels singing....I remember now the feeling of awe which came over me. I felt inclined to kneel on the ground beside the tree where I was standing....I hardly dared to look on the face of the sky, because it seemed as though it was but a veil before the face of God."

"We are parts of a whole," he writes of his moment of vision, "elements in a universal harmony. This, as I understand it, is the 'golden string' of Blake's poem. It is the grace which is given to every soul, hidden under the circumstances of our daily life, and easily lost if we choose not to attend to it. To follow up the vision which we have seen, to keep it in mind when we are thrown back again on the world, to live in its light and to shape our lives by its law, is to wind the string into a ball, and to find our way out of the labyrinth of life."

That string represents, to my mind, both the transcendence and the immanence: something that is "golden," from the world beyond, yet that is also tangible and accessible, within reach, and which serves to tie together my own individual experiences, bind me to others, and pull me Godward.

I suppose it is, for me, both Truth and Beauty, and it is a guide as well as the way I seek to follow in. By pulling and tugging on it, following its twists and tangles in my own life, I acknowledge both sides of the paradox. We are at the same time on the way, dwelling in friendship with God on the journey; and we are going *somewhere*, toward greater unity with God and others, through our choices along the way.

After many years of awe and fascination with aspects of transcendence, following after a sense of longing never fully satisfied in this world, I suppose I have come around the long way to a more immediate joy in the reality of things in themselves—to God in others, to love and friendship on a deeper level—through many meanderings of my soul and windings of that string. It is in the more mature years of our friendship with God and others that we have the opportunity to seek for more balance, the chance to uncover and acknowledge both sides of the paradox more equally.

For essential to any friendship with God is to admit that God's nature is to be both with us and for us—and totally beyond us in holiness and power. Either side of the truth alone is heresy. For if God were merely another name for creation, there would be no real reason to talk about God at all. God would *be* simply *all*. And if God were only immanent, only a friend such as another human being might be to us, then friendship with God would have no dimension beyond earthly love, and prove to be only a metaphor for what we can know of love here.

But Christianity holds tightly onto both sides of the paradox, at times emphasizing one more than the other, the transcendence or the immanence. At times of emphasis on the transcendence there is a propensity toward worship, adoration, experiencing God in the beauty of holiness. Conversely, an emphasis on God's immanence turns us toward Jesus' work, reflected in the Incarnation, in God-made-flesh and come among us. This is the basis for a spiritual vocation dedicated to serving other people in Christ's name.

Acknowledging God's immanence and God's transcendence are both true and necessary to a balanced friendship with God and with others. But we cannot easily experience both truths at the same time, as with any paradox. It is a bit like a picture in my children's "Nutcracker" pop-up book in which slats fold over into another scene: first a come-alive Nutcracker placing the crown on Marie's head; then, when a tab is pulled, the Nutcracker turned back into the boy Hans, startling Marie with his magic. Of course, the two scenes are never seen at once. To know God in both ways, in immanence and transcendence, in a sense of wholeness, we must rely on metaphor, and on the intuitive truth of our own undeniable experience.

Another example we have been using is that of the cross, which, of all symbols, shows us how the two sides intersect. The vertical bar both points and reaches toward God and our mutual relationship; the horizontal bar, forever connected at the center of the whole, both points toward and joins us with other people.

Another example occurs when we begin to look at our lives as a journey, as a metaphor for the progress of the soul. We may at times need to concentrate on the physical obstacles in our way, the stepping stones or stumbling blocks that facilitate or limit our advancement. At other times we go inward, battling within our inner landscape, experiencing our journey as a stretching of the soul. Both are "the journey," yet our limited vision usually gives us one scenario to work with at a time.

Often we have been encouraged to think of our lives as a spiritual journey. But popular psychologist John Bradshaw offers an interesting variation on this insight: "We are not material beings on a spiritual journey; we are spiritual beings who need an earthly journey to become fully spiritual." This is the paradox of our lives and our walk with God, among others.

And this is where friendship comes in. Each of us has particular steps to follow, among others—those incomparable faces that accompany us on the journey. It is through following the path ahead, as we "wind the string into a ball," that we become who we can be with each other and with God.

This book is a coming to grips with some of the consequences of the immanence, a seeking to know more of the friend that Jesus has promised to be to the believer. The more we learn to love, to follow in his steps, to accept the imperfection of ourselves and all those around us to be loved, the more, I believe we encounter Jesus as friend, God as very close and within, as well as far beyond and without.

The paradox of the transcendence and the immanence is never resolved, only lived. Whatever our story is, Christ is in it. God comes to us, reveals the Spirit within us, working at one with our good, and for the good of others. We carry theological truth on the journey. Jesus travels with us. Or as Quaker George Fox puts it: "Dwell in the love and power and wisdom of God, in unity one with another and with God; and the peace and wisdom of God fill your hearts, that nothing may rule in you but the life, which stands in the Lord God."

To know God is also to know ourselves, and thus to be freed to be one among the others that life brings us. It is both to love and to suffer. To Aelred, friendship itself may be equated with that wisdom that is of God: "Since then in friendship eternity blossoms, truth shines forth, and charity grows sweet, consider whether you ought to separate the name of wisdom from these three." Like the wind we cannot see—only the marks it leaves behind on the landscape and on ourselves—so the evidence of true friendship with God is not always easily discerned.

If we are friends with God, will everything go smoothly for us? From Scripture and from the lives of the saints, it is clear that this is not so. Yet so many of the Old Testament assumptions about wealth seem to link it with righteous living and friendship with God, doing his will. God gave much material wealth to Abraham, who was called a friend of God; to Jacob, and to Joseph, whose friendship with God brought him through bondage and near death before material rewards and honor came to him. King Solomon, who asked of God one thing—wisdom—found the pleasure of God's approval. He was given the discerning heart he asked for, and God said as well, "I will give you what you have not asked for—both riches and honor—so that in your lifetime you will have no equal among kings" (1 Kings 3:13).

But the story of Job seriously calls into question for modern, as it did for ancient questioners, the doctrine of retribution, whether being God's friend through righteous living would keep one from harm. Job was tested within an inch of his life, yet he would not renounce his relationship to God. If he could be allowed such suffering while trying to do God's will, what hope is there for us? Clearly there is something more at work in God's plan for the world than an eye for an eye, a tooth for a tooth, or for earthly vindication. We become God's friend not for the honor or reward it will bring us, but through the compelling love of Christ, and for the sake of the unity, the wholeness, that is possible only in him.

We may never see the reward we think we deserve—unlike the happy ending of Job and his final restitution. Instead, it may look to us as though the enemies of God are pretty well off. Certainly the Psalmist thought so: "I have seen a wicked and ruthless man flourishing like a green tree in its native soil" (Ps. 37:35). Psalm 73 speaks of the prosperity of the wicked: "They have no struggles; their bodies are healthy and strong....Always carefree, they increase in wealth. Surely in vain have I kept my heart pure, in vain have I washed my hands in innocence" (vv. 3-4, 12-13). There is a time for the wheat and the chaff to flourish together, and it is not always completely clear to us, especially if we look at wealth and prominence, who is God's friend. Some who cry, "Lord, Lord," Jesus says, never knew him.

Then also there are those who do mighty things, free the captives, heal the sick, cast out evil, and *do not* use the name of Jesus, even of God, in their work. Yet Jesus told his friends the disciples, "Let them be....For whoever is not against you is for you" (Luke 9:49-50). Mysteriously, it seems, some can know God but not call him by name. Are these of whom Jesus says in John 10:16, "I have other sheep that are not of this sheep pen. They too will listen to my voice, and there shall be one flock and one shepherd..." in this enigmatic reference to the unity of all good, the final coming together of all things in Christ, despite appearances to the contrary in this life?

We who acknowledge the golden string, who affirm revelation, who call upon God by name and dare to designate ourselves as "friends of God," seem to possess a certain audacity. We persist in addressing deity, as Annie Dillard has put it, "as though people in themselves were an appropriate set of creatures to have dealings with God." She speaks in *Holy the Firm* of the churches in which the liturgy, the work of the people presented to God, carries an authority and confidence, "certain words which people have successfully addressed to God without their getting killed." Personally, I have never found the roof falling in on our heads as we dared to worship in exalted tones. Rather, it is in mindfulness of the transcendence that we echo each week the words of Scripture for God, our "Holy, holy, holy" a triple reminder of whom we dare to address. Surely there is no more appropriate word for the transcendence, for "holy" has been called the only attribute of God in Scripture that is not metaphorical.

We are ever mindful, through Scripture and any honesty we hold about the shape and nature of our own lives, that God is God, and we are not. Yet we also declare in boldness, "We are his people and the sheep of his pasture." We admit and accept our responsibilities along with our joys in fellowship with the very Creator and Savior of our lives.

If the shape of our lives conforms to that of the cross, then the shape of our experience is surely cut of the pattern and mold. It might be said that in the journey of friendship with God and others, all roads are crossroads.

Herbert O'Driscoll writes in his autobiographical memoir of a childhood in rural Northern Ireland, *A Doorway in Time*, of a hired man, John Brennan, a teller of stories and purveyor of wisdom to the young boy. "Two things I learned from John that I never forgot. About a mile from the farm there was a crossroads. John told me that it and all crossroads were mysterious places. He said that one always had to make a choice at the crossroads and that every choice in some way changed the pattern of one's life. That is why there was an old legend that both God and the devil were very often at the crossroads, waiting. Each tried to ensure that the choice was made that eventually, by many other roads and after many other choices, would bring the traveler to heaven or to hell. One had therefore, he told me, to be very careful at crossroads."

Christ has gone before us as the one who made the choice to die for us. If there is no greater love than that a man lay down his life for his friends, then to speak of friendship is not a small matter, but a matter of eternity. God's friendship with us always includes the cross, the crossroad that Christ faced in his own journey on earth. He became the true friend, paid the ultimate price.

We too are called to the radical friendship with God, with Christ, that our cross-shaped life both bespeaks and demands: to acknowledge the inevitable inconvenience, pain, and suffering with and for others—or to fight and ignore it until its cost comes upon us anyway, unaware. How much better to choose to identify with it, to embrace the cross from the start.

To follow in Christ's steps means always to live with, by, and for others, for that is his way of friendship. Or as Henri Nouwen puts it, our relationship with Jesus Christ enlarges our vision, and "by lifting our painful forgotten memories out of the egocentric, individualistic, private sphere...heals our pains. He connects them with the pain of all humanity, a pain he took upon himself and transformed." He himself is not only the crucified, he is the cross, the crossroad, the shape of true humanity.

How are we to become friends with God? George MacDonald writes, "The love of our neighbor is the only door out of the dungeon of self, where we mope now, striking sparks, and rubbing phosphorescences out of our wills, and blowing our own breath in our own nostrils, instead of issuing to the fair sunlight of God, the sweet winds of the universe."

The cross extends not only upward, toward Christ's relationship with the Father of lights, the God of transcendent good—but also crosswise, toward our neighbor and all that is good but imperfect upon this earth. "Though we do not have our Lord with us in bodily presence, we have our neighbor, who, for the ends of love and loving service, is as good as our Lord himself," said St. Teresa.

Through this view of God as friend, I have become more and more attuned to the fact that the sidewalk outside my house connects to heaven, is in a sense "built in Jerusalem's wall"; that the small, exquisite pleasures I have discovered—the resting of a small hand in mine, or the satisfaction of a writing task accomplished—partake of Christ's humanity and my own redemption in some mysterious way. That even fetching food endlessly, carpooling, dressing small bodies, picking up toys, sweeping up dustballs and sorting clothes all miraculously have their connection to the kingdom. Such humble acts and their satisfactions, or whatever else our work may entail, keep us mindful of our side of the friendship with God we can experience on earth.

The stories that follow are travels with friends that, for me, also taste of the friendship with God in Christ that has been part of my life for several decades. These recollections of friendship are mingled with biblical reflections, occasional quotes from writers who celebrate friendship, and events in my life and the lives of others that coincide with this view of friendship, of "the kingdom coming" in small ways.

At times we experience the pull, know the connection as though the vine could feel the nourishment coming through the branches. At other times it is by faith that we acknowledge that God is with us, that the cord of grace is truly there.

That is one reason for friends. When our faith falters, somehow in God's love, another may be there to close the gap, pick us up out of the mud, do the work that is God's but always comes to us through human hands and hearts. Friendship with God is not only presence, suffering, connectedness, but also joy. In friendship, with and for others on this journey, we are also, in a paradox, brought back into the glow of God's transcendence.

LOOKING AT FRIENDSHIP

1. What is your favorite word-picture or metaphor to describe your view of friendship with God? With Jesus?

   "God has chosen to make known the glorious riches of this mystery, which is Christ in you, the hope of glory"—Colossians 1:27.

2. How does the shape of your friendship extend upward in your devotional life with God? In what specific ways is it reaching horizontally to others? How would you describe the point at which the two intersect?

CHAPTER TWO

My Father, My Friend

I begin, then, with these images of friendship: the clasped hand, the cross-shaped journey, the winding string, and the glory manifest. A memory in my mind's eye begins to tell a story.

A man, a girl, and a dog are walking down the gravelly shoulder of a partly blacktopped road, kicking up dust. It is a short time before sunset defines the boundary of another day. The man is my father, and I am the girl in the picture.

Parents, usually, are there, with and for us, from the beginning. And each parent's way of *being* brings us different gifts and challenges and directs us toward different steps. This image of my father walking beside me recurs again and again as I reflect on friendship in the Spirit.

This particular road we called the "Hard Road," its outer surface being rough and unpredictable—unfinished. Perhaps my father's playful naming of this path, this metaphor out of his multilayered mind, signified more of a description of life itself than I could yet imagine.

I was probably five or six years old when we began our regular walks together. In those days fathers were not necessarily expected to spend "quality time" with their children, especially girls. We were all very concerned about girls being "young ladies," and we held tightly to the expectation that we would grow up to be more or less just like our mothers.

There was no son, no brother in the family for my father to mold in his image. But my father wanted to spend time with me. He welcomed my presence. I had his ear—both literally and figuratively.

This is a strand of the family web of tales, one my parents often reminded me of. It was the time when, as a toddler, I was being carried up on my father's shoulders on a cold Chicago winter day. Always greatly concerned for my well-being, they both suddenly noticed that my hands, which were clinging tightly to my father's ears, seemed to be bleeding. With great concern they checked me for any possible cut or wound, only to find that I had been gripping his ears so tightly that *he* was the one bleeding—his ears unfeeling in the cold.

Such is a parent's friendship in the moment, the forgetting of self in love for a child. I know the feeling on my own, the immense vulnerability of having a child, realizing that you count your own safety and well-being paradoxically more and less because of this connection with your offspring. You want to live better, more intensely than ever before, for their sake. Yet you also know that your life is worth nothing unless you are also willing to die for that child. I felt this paradox, this wound, from the moment of my first child's birth.

Love, the friendship of the Spirit, carries another across passages of time and bears another's burden willingly. It is written in "The Gold Legend" of St. Christopher, he who unknowingly carried the Christ child across a stream, that he laboriously made his way to the other bank and set the child down wearily, saying, "Child, thou hast put me in dire peril, and hast weighed so heavy upon me that if I had borne the whole world upon my shoulders, it could not have burdened me more heavily!" The Child answered: "Wonder not, Christopher, for not only hast thou borne the whole world upon thy shoulders, but Him who created the world...."

A love that is willing to bear another, to suffer another, to be changed because of another, is always in the shadow and pattern of Christ, the Friend whose life has been laid down for us. I believe I knew from very early days that there was a spiritual element to my father's love, to his offered friendship.

I probably thought this was normal, that an intelligent adult could be both father and friend, who expected not only to be there as protector, as far along the road as he could travel with me, but to share this dimension of self-sacrificing love. As a parent he was there to teach me, to point out danger, to offer himself in my stead. But his presence also meant someone to share the insights and the delights with along the way.

What surprises me more now is that he never expected the lessons to be one-sided. He had, not an authoritarian air, but an unusual openness to my *being*, as though he expected not only to instruct me in life, but to learn from me as well. Though he never said it in so many words, he seemed to affirm that I was of value, to God as well as to him and to my mother. And together with this feeling was the strength of loyalty, a trust that I would not disappoint him, and that I would also be true to myself. Nothing could be clearer in the way he has treated me all of my life.

When I think of my father today, now that our friendship has stretched across decades, I realize that his presence with me and for me has created "a small island of certainty" in "the swirling waters of our uncertainties"—as Lewis Smedes calls the committed presence of another person in his book *Caring and Commitment*. "How strange it is, when you think about it, that a mere human being can take hold of the future and fasten one part of it down for another person....We have a mystery on our hands, no doubt about it."

This is a key to understanding Christian friendship that has passed from my father to me. When a parent says, by words and actions, "You are worthwhile. I will be there for you," something in you relaxes, expects, anticipates that there will be relationship, that trust is possible, that you will experience the grace of someone there, with and for you, at each stage of the journey.

This is an insight I think about a great deal with my own children—how my own sense of being in the world influences them, how I am able or unable to accommodate their presence and the presence of others, and how their view of the world is being shaped by my *being*. By my own desire for peace, for a way to live, I guide them step by step into a view that life can be good, that reality can be embraced, and that God is in it.

In this parent-child venture, as in all relationships, we too are Christophers, are Christ-bearers, in all our actions toward others. God is immanent, among us, and to God we are both visible and loved. That is the peace that we are to live in together, as friends. It is a matter of focus, of gazing into another's eyes, one on one, to say, "You are visible, and the sight of you gives me delight." I know, realistically, that with children and their insatiable needs, these are moments that come and pass like flashes of lightning bugs in the summer yard. But they occur, and they matter.

Too often we let these moments pass, dead tired from adult words and thoughts and overwhelmed by the wails of "Read me a story!" "But why, Mommie?" Endless questions. Exhausting demands.

At times like this, my father's patient friendship and accommodation of my presence often springs to mind, and I recover a taste of the gifts of himself he gave me. Sometimes, then, my own strength returns, and I'm able to give a bit more, realizing that even my voice, the searching for the right words, the time I take to explain, to whisper, "I love you" for no apparent reason, is a whisper of Christ through me.

I remember especially my father's word gifts, the accuracy about definitions, about *meaning*, that are a legacy of his friendship. My father and I would always play word games: What two words sound alike but are spelled differently? Which two are spelled the same but mean different things? How many words can you come up with that rhyme with cat? The world of words is like a gigantic puzzle, in which the parts fit in some places, work in some contexts, and not in others. He taught me not a rote inventory, but a *feel* for wordplay, a sense of the rhythm of language and the piercing pleasure when a word hits its target, its meaning, with precision and beauty.

Today I am a writer, and my father stands behind me as a writer's teacher. He sharpened my perceptions, helped me hone my skills, perhaps intentionally, perhaps mostly unaware. For him, part of being a parent-friend was to sense my gifts intuitively, help stimulate my mind, join with me in conversation to sharpen and enliven my engagement with the world. It is hard work, and a choice any parent makes, to invest so in your child—when your own adult mind could easily stick with more "important" things—earning a living, absorbing world news and economics, self-indulgent pleasures, and concentrating on survival.

From my father I began to learn, in delightful ways, how mind speaks to mind, and friend opens up to friend. He created imaginary animal characters for my delight, and told recurring tales of foxes and cats and little mice whose fascinating world always overlapped with our own. As we walked, any mole hole in the path, or hollow in a tree, could easily have opened up to reveal one of these furry friends born of my father's creativity, incarnate in word pictures.

Two of the imaginary characters in his tales were Cleany Fox and Racky Raccoon—names I almost thought too silly to include on these pages—until I recently picked up a copy of the *New York Times Book Review*. There, to my great surprise, I found an article by Janna Malamud Smith, the daughter of novelist Bernard Malamud. She writes: "When I was a child...instead of anecdotes about his father's or his mother's emigration from czarist Russia...he told us about Racky Raccoon, an imaginary quadruped [in a zoo]. Dad cast Racky as a silent comic with a poignant edge: when given two sugar cubes as a treat...Racky happily washed them in his water trough until they disappeared, leaving him puzzled and us enthralled."

My father's own "Racky" stories (which he now tells to his grandchildren) are probably more didactic and, he says, not as clever as Malamud's. But something in the magic of such tales still exists for me, too. It is the personal touch, the giving of a piece of one's imagination to a child, which seems to be part of a larger spirit of creativity that is akin to love.

The particular tenor of my father's friendship was one of love as shared creativity, a fascination with the endless variations and complexities of life (though often with a some-what pessimistic edge), as well as a serious respect for the outer reality of the world. "The relation between the mind and heart of man is a delicate mystery," wrote Owen Barfield, in a discussion of literalness and hardness of heart. The ideal of being hard of head and soft of heart is difficult to attain. Of my father's deep love, I have no doubt. But he was clearly more at home in the realm of the spirit and the mind than in the wear and tear of secular commerce.

A mind that is open to the level of story, welcoming soul lessons in words and actions, is an expansive territory, a world in itself. In my father's receptivity to another's being, to the stories of our own lives as they were unfolding, there was a quality that is the opposite of the binding literalness that Barfield equates with "hardness of heart." The nature of my father's friendship represents the willing vulnerability of the soul, the self-permission to be "got at" by truth, in metaphor and story, even if it requires change in us. It is an openness to God's Spirit, to conviction, to the cross—and thereby, down the long and hard road ahead, to fullness of life.

These are gifts—the sense of a community of spirit, of mind and heart, that I first found a taste for in the friendship with my father. I also recall the blessed freedom I found in the space I was learning to call my mind, and in the world of the imagination—the realm of grace—that my father shared with me.

I am forever grateful that in the community of thinkers, doers—friends of the mind to whom I have found myself related—that my father was there for me. Now that I am a parent, I realize how much more effort it took for him to reach down to my level—how much parents can give, if they choose; and the risk they take of revealing themselves and their vulnerabilities so openly to their children.

Something about being a parent, perhaps awe at the givenness of this life in your care, breeds a kind of recklessness of generosity, a feeling that "this is the place in which I give, if not totally selflessly, then with more abandon than I had thought possible." Thus do caring parents continue to give to and forgive their children, hands clasped tightly; and in these touchings the glory is truly manifest.

My world revolved around both my father and mother, and their roles in the formation of my life have probably been about equal. But it was clear to me early that my father was the one who found thinking, reflecting, and storytelling as pleasurable as I did. These points of sharing and agreement remain part of our friendship still.

In those early evenings, in our dusty steps next to the too-eager dog, Betsy, an atmosphere of ideas and fantastic tales, words, and hopes became just as tangible as the cool air or the dying sun. In fact, I have since learned about myself that ideas from another mind generally get through to me with little interference, while it takes a physical cataclysm to have an equal effect on and change my outer life. I am not as alive to the world of the senses as are many people—nor is my father. We are apt to lament as in the Paul Simon song that we're the "first to admit" and the last to know when something is going wrong.

Of course, being so much alike, we not only enhance each other's gifts—we tend to overlook each other's blind spots. As I give thanks for him and the fact that "I'm not the only one" like this—I also see the bountiful grace of many friendships I've later experienced that are better mirrors of my weaknesses. Each thought like this is a silent blessing of my mother, for her differences that enhance and convict and urge me on to a fullness of personality, as only a different note can help form the richness of a chord.

The resonance of my father is found in his love of metaphor, the expectation of several levels of meaning in any act, the intuitive realization that the life we lead as Christians is not simply an outward journey, but an inward one as well, the steps often coinciding, the lessons overlapping, but the transcendence and the immanence ever part (though he didn't use those words) of his own friendship with God along the way.

My father found his own paradoxes to live by primarily in Scripture, which he read daily. In Amy Carmichael's *His Thoughts Said...His Father Said*, the son "remembered how often at midnight, or in the small hours of the morning when all life's mole-hills become mountains, some Scripture flowing through the mind had renewed his strength. And he knew that in those words was a power that was not of earth." This was the only source of power that he sought.

For my father, these paradoxes, these comforts, were rooted in Christ and mined from his readings in the richest places: from the inner yearnings of the Psalmist, who held fast to God's way, though besieged by enemies night and day; in the wisdom of the Beatitudes, "those who mourn will be comforted," "the meek will inherit the earth"; within the parable of the mustard seed that grows to become the greatest of shrubs; in the day of Shalom spoken of in Isaiah when the lion and the lamb, and all creatures, will dwell in peace.

These paradoxes, truths embodied in seeming contradictions, opened up for him a world of possibilities. They were food for his spirit as well as his mind—for hope that enriched our lives together and brought light in the darkness. Thus did his faith in one small girl—the paradox of inner strength hidden in outer weakness—reside and grow in me, to become the beginning of a vision of adult vocation and fulfillment of gifts.

The seriousness of my father's friendship is a gift that overshadows my remembrances of the inevitable teasing and mirth of childhood, or more tangible gifts such as toys and clothes. In fact, even the gifts he gave had a serious side. I'm sure I never appreciated dolls and their outfits as much as my mother enjoyed making and giving them, nor did I delight in them as my younger daughter, Emilie, does today. But I adored the samples of office supplies my father bought and brought home to help me stock a small desk. They were to me an emblem of actual work in the outside world of adult ideas. At some point he entrusted me with a small stapler—a marvel in those days—that could bind papers together with one clamp, and defied their separation.

Every friendship has its milieu—a place where it can grow and flourish, the tangible setting and props that give interest and substance to the interchanges going on. And for me, friendship's supporting objects increasingly came to resemble office supplies! New paper clips, rubber bands, notebooks galore. Carbon paper! I have no idea at what ages these marvelous staples became part of the story. But the smell of paper, the wonder of that great invention, the ball point pen—the vision of neatness and efficiency with which one could set out to do work in the world was born of these simple gifts and some idea in my father's mind that I could benefit from the tools of mind-work, and share the experience with him, even in childhood.

These lovely objects had use for me then, and promised greater significance later, as school offered me related pleasures: the feel of a new textbook reader as you separate its sticky pages, the pasty smell of mimeographed sheets of homework, assignments that meant I was *connected* with the larger world of ideas and the potential of producing something of value myself someday, perhaps as a writer. How much of this my father envisioned and prayed for, I cannot know. But these delights and tools were eventually to connect me with the world of work where, even today, my deepest friendships are usually found.

How often do we give a friend gifts because we enjoy them ourselves, and we want to build another link of connection, for their sake and ours? The idea of giving me office supplies no doubt came to my father because he himself worked in an office for a large construction company where he held titles such as "expediter" and "field office manager." Surrounded by muscle-work daily, he himself did head-work: correspondence, book-keeping, payrolls, ordering materials, writing proposals to make his bosses look as literate as he was, quietly, behind his desk.

A friend often serves to envision the future with us. And he had greater hopes that I would find a more specialized use of my mind. In fact, his friendship bred in me not only trust in a creative God in whom all things are possible, but a belief in the redemptive quality of hard work, accuracy, honesty, and completing the job. Living in the real world, in which these ideals are not always shared, he probably sought to mold me this way for his own companionship and support as well as my good. And with him, I developed a cynicism toward the "lowest common denominator" of mediocre workmanship to which people often sink.

Yet my father has usually managed (as I hope I do) to avoid the pessimism of inaction that can result in one of his temperament when the ideals don't match the reality. His faith in God's purposes for *him* have largely kept him from despair. And he was never willing to compromise his integrity in order to "get ahead." Though my father would blanch at the word "mystic" and some of its connotations, his inner-directed reliance on the power of the will to sustain belief and endure adversity is a key to his own soul.

If my father offered his friendship as "a small island of certainty" to me in a world that could offer any kind of roadblock at any moment, I did not understand as a child that more than his own will to "be there," with and for me, was involved. Surely my father faced his own crossroads again and again—his stories remain his own to tell someday, or keep. But it is clear from the evidence of his faithful life, today as from my earliest memories of him, that he has managed to stay on the path he chose early in life, one of friendship with God.

Friendship inevitably comes up against obstacles of separation as well as objects of connection. It is a perilous world, particularly where my father worked on a construction site, with accidents poised to happen daily. Deaths were not unknown—caused by mishandled heavy equipment, falling objects, and electrical mistakes. Besides working in the midst of the seeming chaos of a development site, he spent hundreds of hours on the road, commuting through the most heavily trafficked metropolitan areas of Chicago and traveling to far outlying areas in all kinds of weather.

There was also the precariousness of finding and keeping a job (in this he was careful and stable); with the high costs of establishing a family home (he built most of our first house with his own hands); and with raising a child with hopes of "doing better" for her. Thus do the hopes of friendship involve risk and peril for the sake of another. Whatever guardian angels followed my father and brought his current serviceable car home to my mother and me daily are also part of this story. Each day the road urged him on—to performance of duties in a world outside our sphere, but for the purpose of returning to us with the fruits of his labor, a father's way (in those days, not usually shared by a working wife) of nurturing a family.

He braved not only the perils, but the dreariness of it all, the plodding, the willingness to buy security through denial of personal gratifications, year after year. These, too, are the gifts of a true friend. He knew that an initial choice to "be there" must be supported time and again, with the continuing. Perhaps he had alternatives, but they were not readily apparent to him; both risk and glamour were sirens' songs that fell on deaf ears.

There are many ways to journey down the road of life and of friendship, and I respect my father's way deeply. Some of his cautiousness resides in me, too, and like him I take years—*decades*—to allow ideas to take root and start pushing up to the outside world in tentative ways. I prepare; I pray; I perform needed work in the world of other people's lives and expectations. And, like him, I find along the way that friendship in Christ is possible, but it, too, takes time and great effort before the harvest begins to tell.

And friendship engenders hope. Surely the dreams my father planted in me are larger and stronger for the waiting. The legacy of my father's friendship in my childhood is with me still. As my friend, poet Ruth Calkin, has put it, "What God is doing in us now is as important as what God is going to do in us later." We are, every minute, at some crossroads. Indeed, it is all part of the same story.

My opportunities in the world of work and vocation are broader and continually expanding. His only reaction to this bounty is delight in my work, my progress, my adventures.

Children have been compared to arrows shot out from the archer-parent, and if my father stands back from the target, watching my flight, it is as a friend—and with joy—that he gazes ahead. It is I who feel regret that there are places he cannot follow. For I am also an inheritor of borrowed melancholy, of my father's bittersweet outlook on life that is tinged with irony, enfolded in paradox. It is a rich, fertile soil for ideas to be nourished, for those of like minds to find fellowship.

A friend walks part way along our road with us, and my father walks beside me yet, in prayer, in words, in actual steps—in ways I only begin to understand. Not long ago he walked with me and my two children down a semirural road where he and my mother have retired in Tennessee. He and I always resume our lifelong conversation, friend to friend, wherever we are. We fit it in around the distractions of rocks and holes in the road, assaults of nature, noisy traffic—whatever the outer world provides or intrudes upon us.

It is the dialogue of friendship, as particular as our faces. We are winding up the string with one eye on the journey and one on the hope of glory ahead—a commonplace experience, and an echo of eternity.

LOOKING AT FRIENDSHIP

1. Think of specific companions whose "way of being in the world" so nearly conform to ours that we experience true friendship in their presence. Have we told them specifically what the relationship means and has meant to us? Perhaps they don't know or need reminding today that sharing their journey has helped make us who we are.

   True friendship always expects to learn from the other at every stage of the journey.

2. When someone who has been close to us can no longer walk with us in the same way, how does this change our perception of the quality of those earlier stages of friendship? Can we learn to affirm in faith that what did exist for that time was good? Pray for the honesty that is not afraid to claim the joy of friendship as it has been given.

CHAPTER THREE

Mother, Daughter, Friend

M y mother, as well as my father, journeys with me on this path of earliest friendship, but in quite a different way. Mothers and daughters have an obstacle to overcome in finding whether they are or can be friends, what such a relationship will look like, whether it has been forming all along the way, and what shape it seems to take.

That obstacle is their sameness—and their difference. In relationship to one's parent of the same sex, I have found, there are the inevitable expectations of becoming "your mother's daughter" in a way that will make her proud, enhance her own identity in the world. In its best sense, this overlapping identification of a mother with a daughter is a desire for love to extend its boundaries. What begins in the circle of her nurture, she hopes, will carry over to other loves the daughter will encounter as an adult woman.

> love is a place
> & through this place of
> love move
> (with brightness of peace)
> all places
>
> yes is a world
> & in this world of
> yes live
> (skilfully curled)
> all worlds

writes e. e. cummings.

But the style in which this love is expressed, and the territory of the new world into which the daughter makes her way, may seem for years, for decades, to be of a very different shape from her mother's. The inevitable experience of being compared to one's mother, to her adult successes, her more finished personality, the weight of her experience and wisdom in everyday life, is like a shadow a daughter carries with her. It is always there. And it is far more influential and dangerous in her life when she dares to ignore it, deny it, or fight it rather than accommodate it and make friends with it.

The growing friendship I am experiencing with my own mother comes after years of underestimating this truth and finally developing the courage to face our sameness and our differences in the light of day. It entails not only looking at the past, but focusing on the present, too, and on the relationship that is still possible and more to be desired than ever. I am able to be with and for her in new ways as I am discovering how love has its own shape for me. As mother or as daughter (for I am both) means I dwell in that sphere of security and peace that is the gift of God and which the Psalmist describes as very like our early physical relationship to our mother:

> I still my soul and make it quiet,
> like a child upon its mother's breast;
>   my soul is quieted within me...(Ps. 131:2).

This experience of being at peace with my mother's way of living in the world and open to her friendship is both new and warmly familiar. It is like coming full circle, stumbling onto a truth that has been there all along although I had been unable to live in its full presence. Growth into friendship with my mother is something that I can see, looking backward, was there all along. Yet in another sense it is a new thing, as I stand between two generations now, as a parent, a mother of daughters myself. That sensation of reaching toward both generations at once is the crux of what I am learning about friendship—making peace with the side of myself that reflects my mother and with the parts of me that bear little resemblance to the shape of her love.

"Love, the magician," writes author Hugh Prather, "knows this little trick whereby two people walk in different directions yet remain always side by side."

There are steps that women take in their journey, age to age. The first of these is called "awakening," and it is the threshold of a deeper awareness of the Spirit in our lives as women—of our connection with God and other people. This awakening may occur in different parts of our lives at different times, even in different decades. We are never too old for surprises, and this re-awakening to my mother is one that has for me ushered in new understanding and wholeness. For, as mother and daughter, we have been travelers together to this point, out of both necessity and choice.

In my mind's eye, I see us journeying together still, not in opposite directions, but along a large circular track with an inside edge and an outside edge. And while we run in parallel fashion, my eye is turned inward, toward perceptions and intuitions and states of mind, while hers is turned outward, as she keeps a close watch and concern for the world of the senses, the best use of all the material things that present themselves to her unique creativity.

We were talking this morning of the days when she used to do tailoring, redesigning, and sometimes creating clothes for a variety of customers who brought these problem garments (or their problem figures) to her in our home. I had never really noticed, or listened to her tell how she managed to be so successful at it. I knew that she was talented both in dress design (she used to draw professional-looking paper dolls for me) and execution.

She rarely failed to resurrect a garment or find an appropriate pattern to accentuate some positive attribute in any woman. But the process eluded me. Often she was expected to tailor garments to fit someone's changed figure, make good of an ill-fitting dress, or construct one out of the wrong material—when perhaps the better answer would have been to discard the idea and start over. She would lay out her materials, think about shapes and textures, put them away and "sleep on it"—and go to the pile of work when she was fresh for the task the next morning. Through those steps she was always somehow able to turn flax into gold for the demanding customer.

All of this came out as I was discussing with her how I approach the writing process, especially the act of revising an article or a chapter. I, too, gather my materials, pray, reflect, get some general ideas of how to do the thing—and then make a stab at it. In both of our approaches there is that period of doubt, of being inadequate; then a surge of energy and a leap of faith to do the work before us, not in an artistic haze of confidence, but using the practical skills of our own vocations' demands. The sameness and the differences of our lives came suddenly into play. I told her I thought I could understand something of what she had gone through.

The results of our work usually bring surprises, even to us. And to both of our minds, it is grace at work in our individual lives. Her sharing with me how she has worked and arrived at this point, when I had felt so alone on the track many times, renews relationship and further binds our souls in the friendship we were intended to have at this stage of the journey.

We *are* on the same track, a women's path that has included marriage and children and household responsibilities—undergirded by our religious faith and its values. But our interpretation through the years of how to stay on that track has often differed greatly. So much of the work I have "had" to do has been internal, independent, even rebellious, testing new ground that lay in both intellectual and actual terrain far from my mother's world.

Now that we live in closer physical proximity, the spiritual space that seems more one than it ever has before. As books and articles with my name on them have appeared, I suppose I have taken on more of a recognizable identity for her; my work, my years of struggle begin to make some sense in terms of the outer world. Today she both values the evidence of my labor and helps to guard my time and peace that continue to make it possible. This is a legacy of friendship that women who are so closely related—and who thus can painfully rub each other the wrong way, misunderstanding and confusing each other—can experience at this stage of life.

Our differences seem less significant to me now that I am a mother myself, negotiating a much more complex situation than I have ever known. Now I am also deeply immersed in the life of the senses, with many more responsibilities than just earning a living, doing mental work, enjoying adult pleasures. For example, I've joined her in seeing that clothes for the children and me will remain useful through all the seasons, and in fitting physical reality to emotional needs, some of the day-to-day tasks of mothering that must somehow be wedged in and around adult work. And I see, gratefully, increasingly, the many ways in which my mother is beside me, supporting me in the difficult but fulfilling task of nurturing the children given to my care.

It is strange how all the dos and don'ts you heard *ad nauseam* in your own childhood—in your mother's voice—take on a different character when you hear them directed toward your own children. One of the parts I least enjoy about friendship between parents and children is the need for discipline. I have never been a "take charge" person, and I realize now that, very simply put, I do not have the same level of management and organizational skills that my mother possesses and enjoys using.

If I value the strengths of my mother much more today, it is in this practical area, in the discipline and order she sees (with an eye to future effects of present behavior) as a doorway to greater freedom. Sometimes in the presence of my children she sees what I did not see and speaks up. She is willing to bear some of the burden with me, to risk my momentary dislike for her method, and in that way to express her care.

I see this now in the light of friendship. It is an act of far more complex caring than I had realized, as God's care for our discipline and greater good does not always feel comfortable at the time we experience it. This, too, is part of the cross, and in my mother's sureness and her strength of will I see her differently and more deeply appreciate her wisdom as a female friend.

I do not get the same joy she does out of structuring a household or of vigilantly keeping things and people in line. "Stand up straight!" I still hear echoed in my young girl memory, painfully, as though I am always being watched, and my behavior, my very stance, judged continually. I remember the irritation, the chagrin, I felt, or perhaps the sense of failure at having slouched again and been "caught." The Psalmist says that "faithful are the wounds of a friend"—and now, having grown into a healthy posture, I can be thankful for these "wounds." And I understand and care enough to (more than occasionally) irritate my own daughters with similar admonitions, to influence their stature, physically and spiritually. By being willing to be unpleasant, by traveling through an uncomfortable experience together—by negotiating—we all grow.

A friend is someone who cares enough to notice; to stop; to give a word that is true even though it hurts. For the help sometimes comes only through the hurt, the irritation, the temporary estrangement brought about by that correction.

The larger goal, the end result of discipline and caring to guide, is that the child will learn to stand on her own, to grow as she should, to be her own shape, an equal in her own right. "There comes a moment," writes Polly Berrien Berends, in her book *Whole Child/Whole Parent*, "when we let go of everything we think should-be-or-else. Instead...we rest our very lives, on love —just being loving for goodness' sake. Does one lotus blossom get something from the other? Teach the other? Obey the other? Change for the other? No, the long stems of each run to deep roots, and it is the deep that flowers at the surface. And the whole pond is beautified."

Friendship with my mother has, I hope, grown to this point of trust, that the nurturing, with its wounding and seeming estrangement has led to this—to beauty. We have discovered our own integrity—if not at all moments, in part. We have begun to see how our differences complement each other, how respect is part of the definition and shape of love and allows the other to *be*, and to be herself.

Thus, at times on the journey, love serves almost to rewrite the past, or at least cast it in a new light, set it in a broader perspective. And through the years of separation from my mother, of college and young adulthood, as I have forged my own life apart from her identity, I have also grown to acknowledge her gifts and their worth, so easily taken for granted in childhood.

The distance between us seems to diminish as we see that *friend complements friend* if love was there all along: Love, that sometimes almost invisible magician who holds and sustains. This remarkable experience—accepting the enigma of mother/daughter/friend—helps define for me the path of true friendship, and sweetens the journey.

Such truth, so newly in the learning, strikes me forcefully, as at times my mother and I have seemed so different, not only in what we *do* but in what we have *seen* before us—obstacles that have diverted and distracted—and often separated us.

For some women, their mother has been naturally and comfortably their mentor, role model, and closest friend from the start. My friend Jane comes immediately to mind. I have seen an easy being with each other as I have shared in her life with her mother and been in their homes. They have been able to enjoy a compatibility of mother-daughter luncheons and shopping sprees, are usually at one on decisions of clothes and hair. These are everyday graces and conform to many moments I have known with my own mother. Indeed, it is astonishing how much we do share, how she can look at a dress in a store and somehow know that I could use it and that it will fit me perfectly. She is rarely wrong.

But I have also been tempted to envy what I have seen of the way Jane and her mother share in the larger currency of their life, the feel of an easy relationship, an often unspoken, but agreed-on tone or approach to living. I am in awe of daughters and mothers who seem like sisters. To walk so closely with a female friend, to appear to think the same thoughts at the same moment and reach for the same objects with the same ideas in mind—seems an alien experience I can barely imagine. Instead, I seem always to be playing off my mother's tastes in larger issues, voicing the other side to her view, struggling to establish what I really think in order to tell myself—and continue to form myself—in the process.

This is not an uncommon experience for a daughter with her mother; the process does not end or change. The wide divergence of styles we each express in our sides of the friendship have as much to do with our temperaments and inborn needs as with free choice. But with my mother, as is also true with friends who mirror each other more closely, there is a way to go forward, a way to discover how to be in the presence of the other.

For some reason beyond my understanding, my mother and I have always looked at the same thing and seen two different situations, two nearly opposite ways to approach it. I see the tedious work of planning a week's menus and getting everyone fed; she sees opportunities in that for her most creative gifts. I love to read fiction, continually imagining what *might be*; she, also an avid reader, will read only historical fiction, and that only if it is close enough to the "truth."

I love to work independently and am easily overloaded by too many personalities and agendas and demands, while she thrives on the presence of the people around her, the bustle of physical needs and solutions to practical problems in the household. And she is so often unerringly on target in those, her points of expertise. And I, I'm afraid, am often too impatient at trying to explain to anyone the demands I feel in my work, or the half-formed ideas I'm struggling to bring to birth.

Yet here we are, for all practical purposes, friends and confidantes today, as I am in the not-always-comfortable position of balancing mothering with career—a more complex juggling act than my mother ever aspired to. Her desire and her efforts to open herself to my reality, my experience as a woman over these four decades of my life, in which we have pulled apart where the track widened, and hovered close in times of unusual need, blesses me. I see that she is and has always been there for me, too.

Amy Carmichael writes, in *His Thoughts Said…His Father Said*, "The thoughts of the son ran thus: Many friendships are weakening. Perhaps it is better to hold aloof from close friendship and to be content with friendliness.

"His father said, The soul of Jonathan was knit to the soul of David, and Jonathan loved him as his own soul.…'Go in peace,' [Jonathan] said.…'The Lord be between me and thee.'…So the son learned that if only the Lord Himself be the golden bond between heart and heart, all is well."

To rediscover that quality of friendship with my mother is to pick up a strand of that golden bond. Sometimes its name is forgiveness, and always it is love.

My mother has generally been the practical one in our household, forever finding ways of managing things and making her own particular order out of chaos, fitting available materials into necessary space: arranging houses, furniture, meals, gardens, and lives with an eye to making life work, and work well. She is happiest now when her hands are around something— dough for her own biscuits or ricotta doughnuts, material for drapes and children's clothes, needlepoint designs, and just the right accessories for the outfits of the women in our family. She works also with priorities—what to do next, and how to accomplish it all—while we dreamers are immersed in a book or newspaper, bogged in theory. Sometimes those of us around her are irritated by her particular gifts when we would rather let things be! To one who does not feel a sense of urgency to change things all the time—even for the better—the able administrator can be a thorn in the flesh. It is only as the results (usually beneficial and sometimes surprisingly comforting) become evident that peace returns, and it is possible to give thanks again.

My mother is by nature a get-up-and-go friend who has roused me throughout my life to move from one stage to another—how easy it would have been to ignore the signals and dally in old comforts!—just as she is the one who initiated all of our family's house purchases and sales at the right time for profit and common sense. It is in her nature to move on and move out, to hold together while sorting and rearranging life's priorities.

Her results speak for themselves. She is a highly successful woman within her own sphere.

My father never hesitates to give her credit for this, despite the inconvenience and disruption my parents always experience in becoming settled in a new situation. Yet she has never been wrong, and her foresight on these issues always matches our hindsight. She sometimes makes me think of the wife of Proverbs 31 in her enterprise of household management with wisdom, preparing and mending and finding materials; planting and buying. To those of us less capable in these activities, her work is sometimes a mystery. "She is energetic, a hard worker, and watches for bargains" (*The Living Bible*, v. 16)—this certainly describes my mother, words evoking an ancient version of the woman "born to shop"!

"She sews for the poor, and generously helps those in need" (vv. 19, 20). My mother has been a friend of the poor, the needy, the friendless for decades. Her particular gifts of personal and household skills have been put to use in raising more than ten foster children after I left home. She began this vocation late, through an opportunity to give a young girl a home or see her returned to a dangerous situation. Though this post-parenting experience was not directly sought, it led out into making their home a refuge for other girls and gave my mother extended years of exercising her unique abilities.

Countless times she has been called on to buy a whole wardrobe for a new foster child; to establish discipline and make arrangements in the home, in schools; to interrupt her life with late-night trips to the emergency room of the hospital. Once she helped to diagnose a young teenager's rare illness—based on genetic factors she knew of in the birth parents—and helped to save the girl's life. She brought many young, malleable children to her church and Sunday school, introduced them to the previously unknown security of a home in which they would be expected to contribute and obey, but would not be abused or disregarded.

Her legacy in this is immeasurable, for many of these young women could not appreciate what each of us needs to learn— that discipline, too, is a way of friendship, and care for the development of the person the deepest kind of caring. I remember one foster daughter who confided to me that she never even memorized the address or telephone number of the homes she lived in. "I never stay long enough," she admitted, without bitterness. My mother was one friend who was able to induce her to learn some phone numbers and settle in for a longer stay than usual.

She has dealt with other, tougher problems as a friend who is able to disagree and wound, in love, out of her own deeply held beliefs. She tried unsuccessfully to prevent one young girl from getting an abortion, but loved her even through the girl's rebellion and seeming callousness after it was performed. In these and other excruciating episodes in my mother's foster parenting I have experienced, on the sideline, the beauty of a friend who had gifts I might never have seen except in the larger arena of her relationships with others.

Author Joan Gould has written, "We don't have to forgive our mothers their shortcomings as we grow older; we simply join them in coming short." Daughters and mothers—the intricacies of these relationships fascinate me and pull at me from two sides now that I am at the point where clerks in stores call me "madam" and my own growing daughters take on more and more a life of their own. Learning how I am both like and unlike my mother is a task that doesn't present itself at an earlier stage of life.

For me, it has meant growing in other relationships in order to know the friendships of my parents in a new light; stumbling and failing and seeing that my parents' love was still there. Each story of friendship, mother with daughter, is different. I am living mine with new eyes, in new thanks, and in this return I see how my new worlds—of parenting myself, of pursuing my vocation, of growing in love with those closest to me—touch and penetrate that early circle of love and caring my mother provided.

How long, and through what paths, I wonder, will my own daughters travel to find friendship with me? I know that I desire this resting place, amid the struggle, for us all. Will they in different ways ever see me as friend, as I have so recently come to be allied more compatibly with my own mother?

Perhaps they will not easily or readily accept my way of being in the world as their role model—nor, perhaps, should they. What I wish for them, and for me, is that we are willing to stay on the journey, to acknowledge each other's being there, with and for each other, even when that does not seem to be the case.

I desire for them whatever steps are ahead, to fulfill their own ways of being in the world, and I pray for the grace of the letting go that it will require of me to stay there for them, whether noticed or not.

Perhaps we can only appreciate the genius of another's life (particularly that of our own mother) when we are sure of the value and workability of our own. It is at the early stages, when we are trying to find our own authentic style, the proper use of our gifts, our own look and voice, that we tend to judge our mothers so harshly. For example, a friend of mine could never understand her mother's strong desire to be outdoors as often as possible. It sometimes seemed self-indulgent to the daughter, her mother's insatiable need that isolated her from the rest of the family. Then, later in life, her mother told her more of the troubled family she had grown up in, and the freedom she always found when she could get outside and just run in the fresh air, away from the family's squabbles, without the restraint of walls. The physical openness to her was a door of grace, of temporary escape that allowed her to go back and face her situation refreshed.

Sometimes the pieces of others' lives do not make sense to us until, if we wait, they can be shared and contribute to our own understanding and wholeness. What flaws, barriers, wounds will my daughters see to prevent this friendship of two generations? And what graces will be there to make the way smoother, perhaps, than I have known in my own growing up?

"Two persons love in one another the future good which they aid one another to unfold," writes Margaret Fuller. Such friendship affirms that we *can* learn the steps of love, even in this situation, here and now. And if we can learn to love here, in this given place of pain or pleasure, within the familial relationship of duty and necessity, as mother and daughter and friend, perhaps we can learn anywhere.

LOOKING AT FRIENDSHIP

1. Think of relationships that have surprised you at some point—perhaps after long years of thinking you really know a person. What new gifts have you suddenly seen, like found gold, in your friend? Why not tell her, in some way, today, of your appreciation?

   Love unveils itself more and more as trust grows, and eyes are opened to its many facets.

2. Do we love enough to be willing to "wound" a friend, in love, with an eye to greater wholeness for us both?

CHAPTER FOUR

Befriending Yourself

G rowing into friendship with oneself is a facet of spirituality often neglected in the larger topic of friendship.
But if, in the words of Dostoevsky, "to love someone
means to see him as God intended him," then self-knowledge
and a self-respect that is grounded in God's love are well within
the range of our vocation of friendship.

Like many people whose early religious training was strongly
pietistic, I was taught to play down any reference to myself, to
look askance at the self-indulgence of "worldly" people—and
consequently, subtly, to fear truly acknowledging or paying any
attention to the "self" at all. I remember the formula we were
given for JOY. First we were to love Jesus, then Others, and
lastly, weakly, should there be anything left over to give (the implication being that if you were truly giving to those others as
you should, there wouldn't be *much*)—yourself. The lower-case
"y" for "yourself" I substitute intentionally in this simple acros-
tic, for the result was more like J-O-y than J-O-Y.

As with any formula, there is some truth in it, a passing,
healthy reminder to children who tend to be self-centered, that a
life of selfishness is not what God intends for us. But it is
possible to overlearn some lessons.

We should never gasp in horror at the mere mention of the
"self." As Christians who desire to grow in the school of love,
we may need to approach this territory again with a different
understanding of the self, beginning with the goodness of creation. There is a beauty and dignity to the inner person, created
in the image of God, loved infinitely by God, flawed but redeemable. "Then God said, 'Let us make humankind in our
image, according to our likeness'" we read in Genesis 1:26
(NRSV). And to Abraham God later promised, "I will indeed
bless you...and by your offspring shall all the nations of the
earth gain blessing for themselves" (Gen. 22:17-18, NRSV). We

are too quick to remember curse and forget blessing, the very foundation of our friendship with God.

The consequences of forgetting our own creation in God's image is to degrade the self, to fail to claim the blessing and be blessed. If we cannot grasp the goodness of our own lives and honor ourselves in relation to our Creator, we will be unable to honor the unique creation that each person, in all of humankind, represents. And the channels of love and friendship will be obstructed from the very beginning.

There can be no true friendship in the Spirit without a sense of the connectedness of all creation, without some vision of that seamless garment that is *all that God has made* and that is *good*. Perhaps as adults we have too long divided ourselves up in houses and offices, jobs and roles, labeled "mine." We see (and often fight to protect) our separateness, but we have perhaps forgotten how as a child lying in a meadow, we might have, for a timeless moment, felt enveloped by the curve of the sky, buoyed up by the green earth—at one with all things.

Anne Morrow Lindbergh in her poem "Two Citadels" writes:

> We cannot meet, two citadels of stone
> Imprisoned in our walls; two worlds that spin
> Each in a separate orbit, each alone...

but, she continues:

> A child within each house can slip apart,
> Run barefoot out the stairs and out to meet
> His playmate...

Some of us need to rediscover that child, to become open once again to play and the sharing of joy in *all that is*—simply because God made it. The child within, the true self, can only live in acceptance and love, and in concern and regard for other creatures. It is not so much written in books as known from the heart that the universe is the house of God, and our true home is wider than the walls of the world.

But sometimes, when we have been granted a vision of these truths, we find that our task is to rediscover ourselves, to go within. What we are learning from modern psychology about the rights and dignity of the "child within," the inner self whom we must love and *free* to love, is extremely important to an understanding of spiritual friendship. A regard for the loving protection of that self from abuse and harm is wholly consistent with Aelred's classic view of friendship in the Spirit. In a passage of dialogue about goodness in friendship, he warns against any abuse of the self in the name of friendship. In friendship we are to recognize and reject any request from a "friend" that would bring harm or neglect to us, and we must not mask such abuse in the cloak of self-denial:

"For that love is shameful and unworthy of the name of friendship wherein anything foul is demanded of a friend.... As for those who, apart from faith, danger to their fatherland, or unjust injury to another, put themselves at the disposal or the pleasure [control] of their friends, I would say they are not so foolish as they are insane; sparing others, they do not see fit to spare themselves; and safeguarding the honor of others they unhappily betray their own."

This is the light of reason happily applied to spiritual friendship—that anything which betrays the true self, the self of worth that is *known* and *loved* by God, is a denial of that focal point of creation, our own life, in which we inhere. This theological fact should no more be denied when it is applied to appropriate self-love than when it is applied to love of neighbor.

But the pitfalls in focusing on the self, within the art of developing a healthy friendship with the self, are many. There is always the danger of a self-absorption that masks itself as self-love, such as was embodied in the frantic grasping of the "me-generation." And there is a selfishness that is an insatiable hunger, which may hide itself in an obsession with other people and on the surface looks like "love."

The first, the acquisitive, accumulative self, expresses more of an indifference to others and their concerns, or a feeling that there is only so much to go around and I'd better get mine. This kind of "self-love" is both shallow and fruitless; it is ultimately an exercise in loneliness and loss. An example of an awakening from such self-love is C. S. Lewis's character Eustace Scrubb in *The Voyage of the Dawn Treader* of the Narnia books. Eustace, a self-centered, tiresome boy, encounters in the midst of an island adventure a dragon's lair with treasure beyond his own greedy imagination. He grabs at all that he can carry away, coins and jewels, including a diamond bracelet he slips on his wrist. Then he falls asleep. When he awakens with a terrible pain in his encircled wrist, he discovers gradually that he has himself turned into a dragon.

"In spite of the pain, his first feeling was one of relief. There was nothing to be afraid of any more. He was a terror himself now....But the moment he thought this he realised that he didn't want [it]. He wanted to be friends. He wanted to get back among humans and talk and laugh and share things. He realised that he was a monster cut off from the whole human race. An appalling loneliness came over him."

Eustace finds his true self, but not without a painful experience of "unmaking." The lion ruler Aslan, coming to him by night, directs him to "undress." But he has only scales about him! As he learns to scratch at his hard outer surface, these scales begin to come off in layers, like peeling a banana or shedding dead skin after an illness. Each time he sheds one skin, he discovers another hard shell underneath! He thinks, "Oh dear, how ever many skins have I got to take off?" But in the end, only Aslan himself can do the job: "The very first tear he made was so deep that I thought it had gone right into my heart," Eustace recalls to his friends. And indeed such discovery of the true self strikes to the very center of our being, uncovering and tenderly honoring what is there to be found.

The second mask of true love, obsession, greatly involves other people, and thus it often looks to be the real thing. Self-sacrificial, always giving, these people seem to have the "good" of others ever in mind. Yet they are tossed about by a wind of uncertainty and instability when love is not reciprocated, when their dreams are not fulfilled, when they feel unappreciated. This clearly is not the sin of indifference, but neither is it the kind of detachment from others and their controlling effect on us that is a basic necessity of a healthy self-love. This is perhaps a harder kind of mask to shed. Many of us have been taught to give until it hurts, and our tolerance for pain is too practiced to know when we have diminished ourselves needlessly "for others."

One example of self-sacrifice that has stayed with me through the years is the incident in *Little Women* in which Jo sacrifices her long hair, has it cut and sold for cash to help her father, who is hospitalized in Washington. Handing her mother a roll of bills, and with a choke in her voice she says:

"'That's my contribution towards making father comfortable and bringing him home!'

"'My dear, where did you get it? Twenty-five dollars! Jo, I hope you haven't done anything rash?'

"'No, it's mine honestly; I didn't beg, borrow, or steal it. I earned it; and I don't think you'll blame me, for I only sold what was my own.'"

And every young girl reading it probably also asks herself, "Would I be willing to give of my very self like that? Will it be someday required of me?" Sometimes what seems noble (and may be given in the best of intentions) really goes beyond what we ought to relinquish of ourselves and their beauty. It is a sign of coming of age to realize that it is possible to "love" too much.

In whichever way an inappropriate self-love masks itself (and it is interesting that in both cases, something is or must be shed, that the outer condition of the self often reflects the inner), the transformation of self-concern into true self-love is always a thing of the Spirit. It is a breaking open of the shell of ourselves that means rebirth and a radical reorientation in love. Perhaps it does not come without repeated episodes of giving and grasping, shedding and taking away.

Those who have not discovered a way to healthy self-love are still prisoners within a shell. According to the prophet Isaiah, it is the Spirit who sends good news to the isolated—the poor and the brokenhearted—"to proclaim freedom for the captives and release from darkness for the prisoners, to proclaim the year of the Lord's favor…to bestow on them a crown of beauty instead of ashes" (Isa. 61:1-3). I see this as not only a promise to people unjustly imprisoned, to actual captives, but also a dimension of the Good News extended to the prisoners of self.

Thomas Merton writes: "The only true joy is to escape from the prison of our own false self, and enter by love into union with the Life who dwells and sings within the essence of every creature and in the core of our own souls." Such "beauty for ashes" is grounded in God's love, and it enables a discernment of the fine distinctions that are possible between self-obsession (often appearing to be "other-obsession") and a healthy friendship with the person each of us was made to be in the image of God.

We can often tell the difference between self-love and preoccupation with the self when we see them in others, but it is much harder to turn the searchlight on ourselves.

Harry Emerson Fosdick writes: "A person completely wrapped up in himself makes a small package indeed. The great day comes when a man begins to get himself off his hands. He has lived, let us say, in a mind like a room surrounded by mirrors. Every way he turned he saw himself. Now, however, some of the mirrors change to windows. He can see through them. He begins to get out of himself—no longer the prisoner of self-reflections but a free man in a world where persons, causes, truths and values exist, worthful for their own sakes. Thus to pass from a mirror-mind to a mind with windows is an essential element in the development of a real personality."

This freeing of the personality is the work of Christ in us, a breaking down of barriers, and an opening to the light of the reality that surrounds us. Christ said, "My peace I give to you, not as the world gives do I give to you" (John 14:27).

For some of us women, the barriers to seeing our selves more nearly as God sees us have been great. "Barriers to such seeing existed for several centuries in what we now realize were false teachings about spirituality," writes feminist educator Maria Harris in *Dance of the Spirit*. "These teachings said that if a person wanted to deepen her spiritual life, she would have to deny her body and go off to some spiritual realm, untouched by the messiness of material things....

"From this point of view, spiritual life could be lived only by withdrawing from the world...where you had to be *un-selfish*, rather than learn to love yourself....If we made even one mistake we were out of favor with God forever, having to get ourselves back into God's good graces by spending months and years making up for what were actually only human mistakes."

Even though we may have been taught about forgiveness and restitution, there was in this approach to spirituality a nagging embarrassment of being—of being imperfect, being weak, being less than someone else, and a doubting thereby, of *God's being* with us and for us in the moment.

For some of us, being a friend to the self means learning or re-learning a boldness of declaration of God's purposes in all of creation, of daring to accept and enjoy the goodness of that which God has made, including ourselves. This holy audacity of valuing oneself, of affirming both our connection to God and the staying power of this friendship, is affirmed in Scripture.

"Show me the wonder of your great love, you who save by your right hand..." the Psalmist boldly implores God. "Keep me as the apple of your eye." To allow, in such a moment, the personal attention and love of our very being that God extends to us makes us both visible and creative in the world in a way that self-denial cannot.

What happens when the windows are opened in our lives, when the fresh air of our brothers and sisters and their concerns rush in on us, is a richness of complexity in love, in friendship, which was not possible before. Aelred continues: "In His love we possess all things and enjoy fruition of them, finding Him in them all. And thus as we go about the world, everything we meet and everything we see and hear and touch, far from defiling, purifies us and plants in us something more...of heaven." We dare to be, in this life, "friends of God."

We experience the generosity of giving to others that, far from diminishing the self, expands the soul. François Mauriac wrote that "to love someone is to be the only one to see a miracle invisible to others." It is the miracle of the golden bond that exists between us, the love of Christ, and the cord of our redemption.

Sometimes friendship with others is the key, the open door to discovering authentic friendship with the self. This, too, is the legacy of the connectedness of all things. Reaching out to someone else may open out into a maze that winds around until it leads us to the true self. Sometimes, to be healed, we must reach out before we can go within. A friend, says the author of Ecclesiasticus, "is the medicine of life." Aelred expands on this: "Excellent indeed is that saying. For medicine is not more powerful or more efficacious for our wounds in all our temporal needs than the possession of a friend....As the Apostle says, shoulder to shoulder, they bear one another's burdens."

And paradoxically, in this process of becoming other-directed, of seeing that our world is surrounded by windows, not mirrors, the self and its burdens become lighter: "Even more—each one carries his own injuries even more lightly than that of his friend," continues Aelred. "Friendship, therefore, heightens the joys of prosperity and mitigates the sorrows of adversity by dividing and sharing them." Thus we are freed to enjoy not only our friend, but to taste and discover our own lives' goodness again.

It is not a matter of first learning to be true friends to ourselves, and then, as the next step, learning to care for others, turning to friendship as to a new venture. Rather, the lessons of seeing and loving ourselves as God loves us, of accepting, repenting, being refreshed, restored, redirected, continually go on throughout and within our journey among others.

At some stages we need to look inward to a greater degree, to seek the refreshment of the soul that is found only in solitude, prayer, in-gathering, meditation, and deliberate replenishment of spirit. The need for solitude occurs in varying degrees according to a person's temperament or vocation; sometimes it is relative to the stage of one's life journey. Deliberately treating oneself as a friend, as someone worth spending time with, is not everyone's idea of pleasure or gain.

Like any other good gift, however, solitude can be misused. Sometimes the demands of work or the care of others means that we would have to put our own needs first in order to find that retreat and solace we feel we deserve. I have just been through years of carefully weighing how much time I can take "for myself" when the needs of my growing family seemed to fill all the cracks of time and energy I had. There is a case for being the advocate for oneself, the friend that speaks up for one's own rights, in offering oneself the fulfillment of real needs, short of selfishness. It is different for each person, as the need for solitude varies. And often we need a spiritual guide, as well as the wisdom of Scripture—a spiritual friend to help us determine where to draw the line.

I know that when I was able to learn the detachment of letting someone else care for my child for an hour or two, to find the blessedness of uninterrupted prayer, quiet and reflection, of study and then work again—gradually, my sense of self began to return. And it was a more trusting and competent self before God, able to act as well as react. From these lessons, I know that I am a better friend to other people, including family members, when these legitimate inner needs are being met, in the practice of solitude, where God speaks heart to heart.

Theologian John S. Dunne writes in *The Reasons of the Heart*, that "it may be that the water of the inner well is meant only to satisfy spiritual needs, to fulfill the deep longing of the human spirit for God, and not to satisfy simple human needs or to fulfill the simple human longing for other human beings." It is, according to Dunne, the opportunity to learn to relate to others out of a sense of fullness rather than of emptiness. "The will of God is no longer what happens to one but it is something to be done—" as in Jesus' words, "I have food to eat which you do not know....My food is to do the will of him who sent me, and to accomplish his work."

Christ went out to the desert, and there, through enduring temptation and deprivation, found strengthening of his inner self; it was the opposite of passivity or defeat. His experience was a necessary replenishing of the true self before his Father that was to lead him down the path to the cross, to enable him to be the man for others.

"Jesus can say 'I am' in the Gospel of John because his story is the story of the love that comes from God and goes to God," writes Dunne. "Doing the will of God, it seems, means sharing the love with others, relating to them out of the fullness of the love."

Befriending oneself means more than refusing to let others trample on the self; more than allowing self-regeneration, which always benefits others as well. It also means a becoming, the conscious stretching of the soul through the circumstances of life by the practice of *acceptance*.

Vincent P. Collins has written of this self-acceptance,

"Very few people carry a cross of heroic proportions, since God makes each one to measure, and there are very few heroes. More usually it consists of daily annoyances and petty frustrations, disappointment, loneliness, and recurring disillusionment with everybody, ourselves included....The Way of the Cross may be hard, but it remains the only road to happiness, serenity, and peace in this life, on this earth. And at its end there awaits...happiness without measure, without limit, without end."

The limits and borders of the self are as important a lesson to learn in self-friendship as are the joys of self-realization. Our valuing of ourselves as friends leads us back, full circle, to the humanness that may have been so hard to accept, to believe that such failure and weakness could ever beset a friend of God. But that is exactly what we are called to accept. It is that resting in love in the moment, at peace with oneself and God, that engenders friendship of the Spirit, a true beneficence that flows from Christ's command: "Freely ye have received, freely give."

Friendship with the self is part of the divine courtesy God extends to all aspects of creation. Richard Hooker has written: "God hath created nothing simply for itself: but each thing in all things, and of every thing each part in other hath such interest, that in the whole world, nothing is found whereunto anything created can say, 'I need thee not.'"

Thus we are to sing, in the song of creation "even me," no more and no less than others, but "even me"—whether at the altar of communion, or in reading the promised blessings of Scripture, or in our very active lives with others. It is to put in its place an essential piece in the puzzle of creation; to know an important and life-giving focus of friendship in the Spirit.

LOOKING AT FRIENDSHIP

1. What are the greatest barriers you have found to befriending yourself? List five. What specific Scripture passages or words from the saints help you to see the need for a true self-love that enables you to extend friendship in the Spirit to others?

   Go into the desert not to escape other men but in order to find them in God—Thomas Merton.

2. "All things come of Thee, O Lord; and of thine own have we given thee," we pray at the offertory in our worship service. "Even me" is a good addition to that prayer. To what other moments in life can you add these words?

CHAPTER FIVE

Colleagues as Friends: Facing Outward Together

I t has been said that the basis of true happiness is the love of something outside the self. And this is indeed where friendship in the Spirit resides—both within and without us. When we have taken into account God's love and desire for friendship with us and have begun to make friends with ourselves, the natural direction to look is outward.

"We cannot tell the precise moment when friendship is formed," wrote James Boswell. "As in filling a vessel drop by drop, there is at last a drop which makes it run over."

For many of us, it is in our professions, our vocations, that we find others of like spirit, who fill the cup of friendship even as they work alongside us. And if friendship with God is our larger vocation, "the glorious employment of a Christian," as Brother Lawrence has put it, then we cannot help but carry this love into our work. Often the energy of shared labor enables us to bring more to the task than we would have accomplished alone.

I have worked for about twenty years in religious publishing as an editor and writer and have seen, in varying degrees, as in any "world" of work, how this love can be ignored and suppressed, or released and celebrated. Bruce Lockerbie writes in *The Timeless Moment*: "We have not [fully] learned the meaning of the doctrine of Vocation, the significance of the work of our hands in the Kingdom of God...that God's calling Adam in Eden has its parallel in the call given by Jesus of Nazareth."

"He also calls you and me," Lockerbie adds, "to learn from him as apprentice artists in the Master's studio, working and working until what we have made brings glory rather than shame."

We all know moments of embarrassment when the work of our hands does fall short, and times when the end result supersedes anything we ever felt capable of at the beginning of the task. It is in learning these lessons together, as colleagues and friends, that we both embrace our humanness and our limitations, and admit to the grace that is present in every milieu of work, especially when it is consciously dedicated to God.

I see in this call to vocation and servanthood a chance to build between people, as well as to create through the work that is outside ourselves; friendship in the Spirit grows through the potential of the written word and the power of the living Word. And the appeal for me of this aspect of the work is rooted in the concept of servanthood, of laying out one's life along with one's tools of labor. Lockerbie quotes T. S. Eliot in this context: Eliot sees such work as "a lifetime's death in love"—another expression of the Way of the Cross. It is one of selflessness and sacrifice, something both given and taken up freely.

Much of my experience of adult friendship has occurred as I have worked among other people also called to this vocation, who see a dimension in their work other than simply earning a living or writing a book. Rather, by focusing together on God and on the particular expression of the Christian life that is being written about, we are all brought somehow outside ourselves, into the broader world of Christ's will and work. And this servanthood works on two sides: editors serve both their writers, who are struggling to bring something new into the world, and their readers, who will benefit from the ideas, the book itself.

The stories of my friendships with other writers are myriad. I even met my husband through work, "with our sleeves rolled up," as he put it, doing communications planning. Interestingly, some of the other closest friendships I have had seemed to develop with writers who needed my skills as an editor the least. And these writers are often the most grateful for the small assistance I have provided them. Perhaps it is a case of "mind speaks to mind"—our agreement already being so strong that mutual work on a manuscript enhances not only the collaboration, but the relationship.

In *The Four Loves*, C. S. Lewis describes friendship (*philia*) as a love in which people gaze outward at something, rather than focusing on each other, as lovers do. "Friendship arises out of mere Companionship when two or more of the companions discover that they have in common some insight or interest or even taste which the others do not share and which, till that moment, each believed to be his own unique treasure (or burden). The typical expression of opening Friendship would be something like, 'What? You too? I thought I was the only one.'"

When two people of like mind meet, something clicks; a need that perhaps could never even be described before is suddenly becoming tended, like a crack being filled, and the experience of synchronicity, a unity of purpose and action, is achieved. Often it is a way of *being*, of being with another, a sense that someone asks the same questions as you do, with the same intent, and that you will find both a stimulation of interest in whatever you are looking at together, as well as a comfort and richness of appreciation that satisfies an old longing for home.

I think especially of my friend Anita and her way of being there with and for me. She is a friend whose difference from me somehow enhances our sameness, so that we can begin our conversations always at a point of both comfort and delight.

I first met her early in my career as an editor when she and her husband were speaking at our publishing company, relating their travels in the Soviet Union. I was a new editor, looking for stories for a teen magazine, and slightly overwhelmed with the task of filling up a year's blank pages of my magazine, a quarter at a time—many months in advance of publication schedules.

I needed good nonfiction stories, well written, with reader interest. How would I approach her to find out what she could offer me?

As it turned out, after her talk, she took the initiative and promised to send me a first-person interview with a young Russian girl, whose testimony she had related. When it arrived, on time, in our offices, it was beautifully written and right on target. We printed it and received more Letters to the Editor on this particular piece than anything else that year. It was an instance of grace with mutual benefit, as longer pieces with her byline began appearing, and her work later grew into books. She also made me look good, as her editor.

I know now that the business part of working together—moving words along to the right audience, making connections—all were part of the initial friendship that bloomed from our first encounter, somewhat to my surprise. But more than that, as the years have passed, a compatibility and ease of sharing in our personal lives has only grown stronger.

We ended up taking graduate degrees together, which brought us more companionship and a chance to study writing under Madeleine L'Engle. Our shared classes and masters dissertations gave us welcome forays back into adult learning, and degrees that sent us, better equipped, back to our vocations.

Anita and I still consider ourselves "sisters" today, our friendship solidly based on these shared experiences and sensibilities. We often end up sending letters that cross in the mail because we have been in each other's thoughts at the same time. She is a wordsmith herself, who shares her editorial gifts with her office mission staff as part of her vocation. She often surprises me, introducing me to new words, new concepts and ways of relating others' stories of faith and courage. These are some of her gifts, along with a mature perspective and years of study that qualify her to be a commentator today on the rapidly changing situation in Eastern Europe.

Knowing her is an education in itself, a stretching of my own interests accompanied by a delight in her company. The "thing" outside ourselves that we love and help each other enjoy is theology beautifully expressed, the wealth of Russian literature— Dostoevsky, Tolstoy, Berdyaev, Bulgakov, Divomlikoff—and the expression of faith found in Russian Orthodox theology, which is a branch of literature itself. Our mutual interest has led to a sharing of books and ideas, sending each other quotes and articles regularly—and once to the formation of a small study group of other Russian literature devotees.

When we get together after long or short absences, we always pick up where we have left off—being essentially our same selves, despite the experiences we've undergone separately. Anita is a friend whose essential being makes me view the world as a more friendly place. She is also a friend who has courage, who repeatedly takes risks in her travel and work with Christians in communist countries. Frequently she has experienced the deliverance of the Lord in the midst of peril. The call of her vocation is sure, her "glorious employment" in the work of Jesus of Nazareth.

In my friendships with other writers and editors, I appreciate the connections, the shared effort, the collaborations. But for most of us there is another dimension that buttresses friendship and gives it its richness in the moment. It is the solace of independent work, of solitude and its labor, that occurs in a rhythm of alternation with planning meetings and group efforts that are also part of the publishing process. Psychoanalyst Anthony Storr, in his book *Solitude*, writes: "Two opposing drives operate throughout life: the drive for companionship, love, and everything else which brings us close to our fellow men; and the drive toward being independent, separate, and autonomous." In the work of editing, writing, publishing, I have found a felicitous mix of independent labor and work among friends of the mind—and heart.

Looking outward together, at work to be done, is a great equalizer, a steadying influence. Factual, objective content, as well as personal ideas, give a context to friendship and shared tasks. And in the field of Christian publishing, there is the added dimension of producing books for spiritual inspiration and devotional help. Like any imperfect endeavor, it sometimes succeeds.

In most office situations, editors work quite independently in their cubicles, with a phone handy, and perhaps a few consultations a day with colleagues, authors, or other departments. They may work closely by phone and through correspondence with an author whom they never meet in person. Copyeditors, especially, go about their ghostly business with seemingly little outside contact with others.

It is amazing to me how many rich friendships have occurred over the years among those self-contained spaces. One reason is that any print-work has its limit—on the eyes, the mind. There is the tedium of proofreading that demands a silly break. An article or a cartoon in a magazine you've just read just begs to be shared. And wordsmiths like to talk—need to talk—some more than others. So the conversation, when it does occur between cubicles, is sharp and concentrated, like the lead of a mechanical pencil shaping up a work. Francis Bacon writes that a friend's "wits and understanding do clarify....In the communicating and discoursing...he tosseth his thoughts more easily; he marshalleth them more orderly; he seeth how they look when they are turned into words; finally he waxeth wiser than himself." Those "interruptions" when we just need another human voice to contrast with our own, are often more than self-indulgence or lack of dedication. They are a necessary stimulus to continuing at our solitary tasks with sanity and precision.

The balance of solitude and exchange I have found among friends at work has provided a wonderful basis for friendship that focuses on outward things and not on changing each other. After all, editors have something else to work on—the all-important manuscript itself.

Friendship among colleagues has a cleanness we cannot achieve in family relationships, however nurturing and loving they might be. We generally leave our colleagues at the office along with the work, or at best pick up strands of fellowship when we meet them at other places. There are limits to every friendship, and often the work itself and concern for its benefit helps us set and keep such guidelines of noninterference.

But the moments of connecting, idea with idea, friend with friend, can be very rich and satisfying when they occur. I still share copies of my current writing projects, before publication, with my colleague Wright, who seems to have that eye for what I was trying to say but didn't realize myself. He gives his seasoned advice freely, with an eye to recognizing the underlying truth, as well as the limitations in our ability to express it. George MacDonald has written, "One difference between God's work and man's is that, while God's work cannot mean more than he meant, man's must mean more than he meant....A man may well himself discover truth in what he wrote; for he was dealing all the time with things that came from thoughts beyond his own."

Wright does not find it unusual that I pray over my typewriter at the onset of any new work—and now over my word processor. So does he.

Through the years, as we work with people whose eyes see what we see and whose skills bend in the same direction as ours, our fondness for them and their uniqueness usually grows. I think of Jennifer often now that she has retired and I rarely see her, and how her presence as executive editor was a kind of Central Office of Information and Standards when I worked under her. What is interesting to me is how a business relationship became gradually more relaxed, more personal, through our correspondence. We send each other family pictures each year, notes and well-wishes, woman to woman, despite our difference in ages and circumstances now.

Colleagues are to us a living milieu, their presence and shared labor far more influential in who we are becoming, alongside them, than we can perhaps comprehend day to day.

I never felt this loss of stimulation and companionship more than when I "retired" into motherhood after fifteen years of working in an editorial office. As I continued to work at home, I had the same sorts of tasks in front of me, kept disciplined hours, and produced work on time. But there was often no one around during the day to break the silence (as I also waited and prepared for the birth of my first child), to show me a clipping or joke or pop into my office with cookies or the newspaper.

Those of us who work primarily independently may think we are more self-sufficient than we really are. I wrote my first book in those early months of adjustment. And the silence, the solitude and reclusive atmosphere is palpable in those pages as I tried to make good of the absence of collegial friendship, even while surrounded by other loves and lives in a city parish family. The friends of our workplace may not always be directly involved in our thoughts and actions as we labor at tasks, but even their physical presence, I have found, is a sign of community and a force for equilibrium, restraint, discipline, and joy. The presence of others, with and alongside us, with similar goals and loves, is also a sign of life on the journey. Work brings an added dimension to friendships as well, a delight of order to the mind that loves some familiarity along with the excitement of change. I have missed my colleagues greatly in the uneasy transition to the even more independent work of writing for a living.

With several of my colleagues through the years I have shared a love of poetry and fiction, theory of language, and the arts. My friend Ben always had an eye for the quote or new book, clipping or cultural event that would add spice to long print-filled days. His shared interests brought refreshment to me in my work, helped me keep my own creativity alive, and reminded me frequently of the world of ideas outside our office. Just to say to a colleague, "I like this too; it's just our interest," is to share the friendship that looks at an outward good and increases inward joy. Such are the moments that help connect friend to friend.

Friendship that grows within the straits of shared work can not only help break down the barrier of loneliness, but keep you on your toes and even spark ideas that will blossom into further creativity and vigilance.

With the friend who gazes outward alongside you there is the potential for bringing something new into the world, a product or idea or a correlation of methods that didn't exist until two agreed on something, until a collaboration for something good was engineered outside the self. When this occurs, in the excitement of shared labor, there is for a moment or longer a forgetting of who contributed what to the result, and only joy that progress was made, something accomplished, a task completed. I felt this especially when I was an editor planning and developing new curriculum products. I worked with my friend Kathy, a writer of children's curriculum, to help her find the courage and discipline to tackle a large project, a complete visual aid packet. Her gifts at visualizing and making models of the packet contents were exciting, and with my encouragement and a few suggestions and ideas—it all worked. New songs, new puppets, new stories came to life for teachers to use in classrooms around the country. We needed each other to help bring the packet to birth.

For when friendship occurs in the midst of collaboration, something new appears, becomes visible as a sign of love reaching out. Focusing on what two can do better than one allows a release from the self that is an important aspect of love. "Work is love made visible," says Kahlil Gibran in *The Prophet*. "You work that you may keep pace with the earth..." and with the needs of others for whom you are responsible.

And in this milieu of friendship you also learn a way to keep stride with each other. For there is a rhythm to such friendship in the Spirit, when the worker, valuing the task, can for a moment see his own toil as an image of the Creator's own hand in making the worlds. The task of Adam, of naming and valuing, of joy in the particular manifestation of God's creation, goes on in us. "In the case of man," writes Nicholas Berdyaev in *The Destiny of Man*, "that which he creates is more expressive of him than that which he begets. The image of the artist and the poet is imprinted more clearly on his works than on his children."

The bringing of work to birth—I speak not only of production of ideas into finished form, but of any worthwhile labor that yields results—is part of our human task. When touched by the Spirit, it reminds us of who we are, and who we are becoming, by, with, and for each other. The method through which such companionship in work expands into friendship is through dialogue—conversation. Sharing our minds and hearts, we affirm that the lively stirrings of soul to soul can be captured, to a degree, in language. We affirm by faith that such communication is possible, and we act on it in a leap of faith, sharing in the spark of life between God's hand and Adam's.

It is in these friendships that go beyond casual chat and intermittent contact—in relationships built on work and serious contribution to life—that one comes to recognize something of the joy and terror of being human, of being co-creators with God and with each other. We come to see our very placement in this circle of friends and workers as quite beyond us, part of some plan we can only infrequently glimpse, intended to nurture us and our gifts for the building up of the kingdom.

The story of how I got my first editorial job involves just such a circumstance and placement quite beyond my plan. When I was in college, my mother happened to be working part-time in a small dress shop in a neighboring town. This shop happened to be next door to a Christian bookstore, which she visited from time to time on her breaks to look for Sunday school helps. One day she found herself in conversation with an executive from the Christian publishing house that owned the bookstore. She decided to put in a word for me, telling him I wanted to be a writer and editor, and in a roundabout way suggesting they hire me for the summer in the bookstore. He did her one better. He called the editorial offices in Chicago and lined me up with my first job as an editorial assistant.

I began to learn professional proofreading—and from there, began my first stumbling attempts to edit old out-of-print editions of books into new formats. My editorial career was born, with experience and references to carry me into my full-time vocation after I graduated from college. I was able to gain continual exposure to "what makes a book," as well as how to improve one through precision and careful thought.

Dorothy L. Sayers says that "the only Christian work is good work well done," and this has been my belief, too, as I have traveled a vocational path with friends of the written word for the last twenty years. I am most grateful that the road of friendship for me has included many colleagues of whom I can say, "Iron sharpeneth iron;/So a man sharpeneth the countenance of his friend" (Prov. 27:17). Such friendship, of challenge and delight, has been for me a bridge to happiness that is a love of something outside the self.

LOOKING AT FRIENDSHIP

1. How have the circumstances of your own life's work provided the basis of friendships?

   Think of ways in which our work enables us to become who we truly are, and how friendships are allowed to deepen in that process.

   Facing outward together draws us closer to each other on the journey of friendship.

2. When I pray for friends with whom I have shared tasks, I will envision and offer up their work, also, as I value them before God today.

CHAPTER SIX

A Song for Kathy

"Great friendship is a delight: a hyphen between two minds, a bridge between two wills," wrote Elizabeth Selden. These words, these thoughts, are a song to celebrate such a friend, who once walked closely beside me. As we travel further in the years of our journey among others, nothing is more natural than that we will encounter not only love along the way, but also that untimely intruder, death. Several years ago I experienced the loss of a soul-friend named Kathy, who had, for much of our concurrent careers, shared not only my dreams and hopes—but the pleasures and pains of day-to-day work as my office-mate.

I have lost several colleagues to death through the years, and each time it is a shock that something so natural and given as comradeship could be snatched away overnight. After the awful news, the reality of loss, it seems that the familiar, vacant physical space—a room, an office, a corner of the world that once held a friend's presence—suddenly becomes the emptiest place in the universe.

Grief, the mourning of what once transpired in this air, of conversation and exchange, lingers as a tangible reminder that we do indeed, in this life, "mingle with immortals." Day to day, we share space and words and hurts with beings whose destinies lie beyond anything we have yet seen along the way. We stand at empty doorways, on the thresholds of their departure; but no one ever comes back to reassure us, to comfort us. "Friendship is the shadow at evening," wrote Jean de LaFontaine, "it grows until the sun of life sets."

Kathy and I became friends during college days when I found myself assisting in the travels and stage set-up for a small drama group of which she was a member. We could hardly have been more opposite. I was shy, reserved, and serious; Kathy was spontaneous and bright, an actress who brought dramatic flair to her parts, as well as costume and makeup experience to the troupe. It would have been difficult to imagine then that we would ever become such close friends. But love has its way of overcoming barriers, of being willing to complete what another lacks, and to call it friendship.

These were early stages of reaching out, for us both. My boyfriend at the time, one of the actors in the troupe, was admired by several of the other women, and this tie could easily have been a barrier, a point of jealousy, preventing friendship. But with Kathy and me, a friendship of women opened up, a sharing behind the scenes, a valuing of each other. Exchange occurs on many levels in many types of love. As Kierkegaard says, "When one has once fully entered the realm of love, the world— no matter how imperfect—becomes rich and beautiful, for it consists solely of opportunities for love."

Kathy and I always kept in touch. She became an editor, too, and eventually worked, partly through my suggestion, at editorial jobs at the two publishing houses where I worked. We kidded about how she always ended up following me, and whatever I did, she would do next. But in reality we were very different in our approach to our work—as we were in our style and expressions of love. In our case, the differences brought respect, a willingness to learn, and through the years, a deep sharing of our personal, as well as our work lives. Perhaps it was our differences rather than our similarities that constituted our gift to each other.

When Kathy died of cancer in her thirties several years ago, it was not my friend who seemed changed, as C. S. Lewis wrote at the death of his friend Charles Williams, but death itself. There is an overlapping of the space between us, a contact between us still in silent memory and the sting of absence, that is forever part of my own journey. I simply cannot imagine life in the Spirit without Kathy—who she was and is yet becoming in those "vast fields of experience" (that beautiful phrase of Evelyn Underhill's) that await the soul.

Simply to reflect on Kathy and her gifts is to reach for poetry. If I am the moon, part shadow and part light, then Kathy is the sun—full of presence and light in all her aspects—sunny in outlook, in disposition, in demeanor. My movements are quick and my mind jumps from idea to idea. I ponder and reflect. She used to tease me about the Peanuts cartoon in which she identified with Charlie Brown who saw only a duck and a horse in a cloud formation, while Linus saw a map of British Honduras, a profile of Thomas Eakins the painter, and an impression of the stoning of Stephen!

She endured my esoteric tastes with good humor and a healthy respect. But Kathy helped me learn how to slow down and live more fully in the present moment, in a greater fullness of both mind and heart. Her own sharp skills of thinking were comfortable to her, and her enthusiasm for the most mundane to the sublimest pleasures of life—from a bag of candy at her desk to a classical concert—was contagious. She was always able to induce me to look around, to take time to see what was there—in the world and in the beauty of other people—to smell the flowers, to enjoy, and to acknowledge the Creator's hand in all of it along the way. She seemed to know instinctively that setting mental goals and accomplishing work is fine and necessary, but *getting there* is not really the point in life—rather it is traveling with joy and thanksgiving along the way.

As I just picked up a letter Kathy wrote to me during a remarkable period of her remission, I see unmistakably in her large, open script her embracing of life even while great shadows hung over her health, her spirit. "I may be speaking at church to share my story," she wrote. "Pray it will advance the Kingdom, OK?" I reach even now for a pinch of her courage in those words, her prayers—so other-directed, despite her own painful uncertainties.

In my mind's eye I hardly ever see Kathy alone; she is always, as she was in life, surrounded by other people, not as a queen bee holding court, but as a participant in activity, a key contributor to a vast web of relationships, being Kathy in her own unique way. Her friendship was never exclusive but always seemed to welcome another in, while slighting no one who was already there. She loved to get her friends together, based on mutual interests that she was always discovering and relaying. She was never selfish about them, not needing to monopolize, but able to echo in some fashion the words of the blessed in Dante's Paradise: "Here comes one who will augment our loves."

C. S. Lewis writes in his novel *The Great Divorce* of a lady in heaven in whose honor bright spirits dance, scattering flowers. When the narrator strains to find the identity of such a person, he is told: "It's someone ye'll never have heard of."

"'She seems to be…well, a person of particular importance?'

"'Aye. She is one of the great ones. Ye have heard that fame in this country and fame on Earth are quite different things.'

"'And who are these…dancing and throwing flowers before her?'

"'Haven't ye read your Milton? *A thousand liveried angels lackey her.'*

"'And who are all these young men and women on each side?'

"'They are her sons and daughters.…Every beast and bird that came near her had its place in her love. In her they became themselves. And now the abundance of life she has in Christ from the Father flows over into them.…It is like when you throw a stone into a pool, and the concentric waves spread out further and further. Who knows where it will end?'"

When Kathy and I shared an office, it was full of people, not to see me (unless there was specific business or a single close friend nearby, which is more my style)—but to see her. Because of her openness to another's reality, her many talents (speaking, sewing, writing, crafts, fashion consultation) were invitingly accessible to others. I think of her often, sitting with some unusual handiwork in her lap, knitting or embroidery or needlepoint she had just finished—or sometimes only half-done but wrapped just so for the person receiving the present. You knew she would get it done eventually.

Her priority was other people. "I want to be known most in life as someone who loved those close to her…not by anything I accomplish," she once told me, not long before the insidious signs of bone cancer were discovered by her chiropractor when she finally went in for recurring back trouble. That discovery— the doctor himself drove her to the hospital—began for her an excruciating journey that some of us shared as best we could. She traveled back and forth through remissions and hope, and was struck time and again by recurrences and reactions to necessary treatment that put her in and out of hospital care, with no end in sight.

"God is teaching me some big lessons...about *choosing* to obey *every moment*—in small things as well as large. Learning to focus always on his perspective," she wrote. I was able to send her my first published book just before her death. I had left my editorial job by then and moved with my family from Illinois to Ohio, so I was not around during the final months of her ordeal.

She wrote, "How you find time to write with your two little girls is a mystery to me! You've always been a disciplined person, though."

I'm not sure that when I wrote my chapter in *Awaiting the Child* on "escalating grace," I did not have Kathy primarily in mind. I said, "The more we are able to face death—our own, others' we love—the less, I believe, we have to fear. I am convinced that there are graces yet unknown to us, because they are not yet needed." In her last letter to me, weeks before her final coma and death, she wrote simply, "Pray that I'll have the grace to be patient and take what is ahead...."

Kathy is not only friend to me in the fact of her acceptance of me, of having been alongside me through these stages of her life, but also by her example of endurance. If it is at all possible to "make a good death," Kathy taught us how, as she endured the continued onslaught of treatments and tests and tubes and pain and loneliness, through a passage that her husband, daughter, parents, and friends could not follow. How they longed to take more of her burdens, if only it could have been possible. Her father once told me, as we waited in a hospital lobby, that he would sell all, give it all to Kathy, if only he could bring her back to health.

Connected to Christ, we are connected to each other—that is one lesson that is a legacy of her life and death.

The last time I saw Kathy, my husband and I visited her in her city hospital room on a dark Chicago night. As she finished up her evening meal, we hugged each other, as always. But even then, before any outcome was certain, I perceived in my sunny friend a level of gravity to which I, in all my serious demeanor and introspection, had never come close. She faced us, but I sensed her spirit already faced another direction, toward a world of greater light and permanence. She was becoming, already, more herself, more prepared for that City (in that heaven of *The Great Divorce*, even the blades of grass are firm and can hurt unaccustomed feet).

Perhaps for her a door had appeared toward that other side, a crack revealed, only to be shut again as she returned to the travail (from the same root as *travel*) of her earthly life. I said nothing of my perception, but I sensed a difference, a taking into account the either/or nature of our sojourn: "For me to live is Christ...to die is gain." Somewhere in the tension between those two possibilities, she even then had found peace.

When we left the hospital, I saw reflected again in the many brilliant lights of the skyscrapers around us a glint of the City, for it was as though heaven touched earth in that moment. It seemed that the state of being in oneself, the peace that is possible in any circumstance—"Choosing to obey *every moment*"—was granted to her, and for a moment, to me.

Thus do friends open and show us doors and windows we might so easily have avoided or missed. That was the gift of Kathy's presence by and with us, for such a few short years, it now seems. All the possibilities and opportunities of love indeed can, in an instant, be mirrored in one face. I will never forget her radiance that night, as one light in the City never to burn out.

If ever I doubted the truth of the existence of a life beyond this one, of connections between friends that are a matter of eternity, Kathy would instantly quell doubt in me. Though her body could no longer sustain her, her presence has forever touched my life and I can no more imagine the end of Kathy than of the sun. Even on clouded days, though we do not look directly at it, we see by its light.

LOOKING AT FRIENDSHIP

1. Friends present and absent from us physically may be part of us in ways we only begin to comprehend. For what friends can you give thanks as you see them in retrospect?

   Friends teach us that longing for more than we have yet seen or heard or experienced.

2. What have you learned from friends who were different from you but willing, graciously, to make their gifts accessible in your life?

CHAPTER SEVEN

Man-Woman Friendships

"What is a friend?" wrote Aristotle. "A single soul dwelling in two bodies." Probably in no other type of friendship are we tempted to expect such metaphysical unity in love as we do in marriage. For in the freely chosen union of marriage, the oneness that occurs includes the physical joining of our bodies as well as other aspects of our personhood—indeed, of our spirituality. Urban T. Holmes writes in a chapter on "Sexuality and Holiness" in *Spirituality for Ministry*:

"Sexuality encompasses a person's mind, spirit, and emotions, as well as his or her body. It is impossible for us to meet someone else except as a sexual person, just as we cannot meet another except as a spiritual person." Or, as Holmes quotes one priest who is asked about his sexuality: "Sexuality is the expression of the whole personality, as I understand it; so is my spiritual life."

Thus the idea of a marriage of opposites, of man and woman in soul and body, expresses our deepest hopes for wholeness and unity in this life. Because of this gravity and potential, often rational explanations break down, and sometimes only myth can come close to touching the depths of this common human experience and desire.

In Plato's *Symposium*, the myth of the unity of the original human being is explained by one of the characters in the dialogue. The original being was a spherical creature with two faces looking toward opposite directions. Each being had four arms and four legs, and thus represented a kind of perfection—so much so that the gods were jealous and split them cruelly into two halves. And ever after, it is said, the two lost parts seek eternally to reunite and again form a whole.

I first encountered this myth referred to and illustrated on the playbill cover at Stratford-on-Avon, where I once saw the

Shakespearean play *Pericles*. It offered a beautiful representation, in glossy sepia print, of this creature, with the implication that the play itself was an enactment of Plato's truths in a human love story. I remember that the visual and the philosophical together stirred my imagination and served to shift my understanding of the play itself to a more universal level.

Of these creatures Plato said, "When one of them meets his other half...the pair are lost in an amazement of love and friendship and intimacy." Scriptural teaching on marriage in some ways also evokes this myth, the idea of man and woman becoming "one flesh" through the commitment of vows and the uniting of their lives for a lifetime. In Genesis, however, in the context of the creation of Adam and Eve, the woman is shown to be separate and whole, but generated from the rib of the man. It is further explained that "this is why a man leaves his father and mother and joins himself to his wife, and they become one body" (Gen. 2:24).

Many of these allusions offer an appealing invitation to the "ultimate" friendship, a fulfillment of mind and body, a union of souls. And the experiences that some couples have in marriage at least reflect shades of the possibility of such unions on earth.

In her novel *Nuns and Soldiers*, Iris Murdoch describes Guy and Harriet, a couple in their forties facing the imminent death of Guy, the husband, and offers this poignant and somewhat ideal yet believable view of a marriage:

"They had always been very close to each other, united by indistinguishably close bonds of love and intelligence. They had never ceased passionately to crave each other's company. They had never seriously quarreled, never been parted, never doubted each other's complete honesty....Their love had grown, nourished daily by the liveliness of their shared thoughts. They had grown together in mind and body and soul as it is sometimes blessedly given to two people to do."

Another joyful example of a couple's experience of such a partnership is found in Madeleine L'Engle's *Two-Part Invention: The Story of a Marriage*. She writes of her years of friendship in marriage with the actor Hugh Franklin. It was a long love affair that began in romance, and was cemented through the years with commitment, good humor, and their recognition of God in the partnership. The night that Hugh proposed marriage to

Madeleine, she relates, "he suggested that we play records, and chose Tchaikovsky's *Swan Lake*. He picked up a book of poetry off the shelves and began leafing through it, and then read me Conrad Aiken's beautiful words: *Music I heard with you was more than music/And bread I broke with you was more than bread.*"

When the friendship that is love begins in romantic attraction, man to woman, and woman to man, often there are intimations of the larger strains of music and poetry, a generosity of spirit, courtesy, and strength, in one or both persons. Whatever archetypes appear, even fleetingly, to the imagination help to bring the individuals into a sense of something beyond themselves—to love, transcending their particular circumstances, yet drawing them into its beauty, creating something new that has not lived before. Almost a new creature.

"In Friendship...," writes C. S. Lewis in *The Four Loves*, "each participant stands for precisely himself—the contingent individual he is. But in [*eros*] we are not merely ourselves. We are also representatives. It is here no impoverishment but an enrichment to be aware that forces older and less personal than we work through us"—the masculine and feminine aspects of our own souls that transcend us.

These masculine and feminine "forces" are powerfully evidenced also in Scripture, particularly in the Song of Solomon, in which the delights of human sexual love are celebrated—and the joys of God's courtship of the believer are also intimated. Both of these strands of love, human and divine, are built into the nature of things; and it is as impossible to sort and separate them out as it is to take apart a rose to discover its secret.

In Christian marriage, the ultimate friendship, it is wise to seek awareness of these truths and then simply to live in the richness of this perception through the demands of everyday life. Happily, in Madeleine's and Hugh's case, a love born in mutual delight also shared work in the theater world of New York and a belief in the sacredness of their marriage vows. It led to many years of happiness until Hugh's death of cancer in 1987. L'Engle wrote earlier in *The Irrational Season* of one of the secrets of preserving both the individuality and the togetherness that she and her husband enjoyed through the years:

"Somehow or other, Hugh and I have managed to be guardians of each other's spaces—most of the time—and because of

this the spaces between us are not chasms, but creative soli-
tudes. When we blunder, then the spaces are horrendous and
solitude turns into the most painful kind of loneliness; but then
a willing acceptance can turn the loneliness back into solitude."

Between the points of these romantic and practical assess-
ments of a friendship within marriage lies a lifetime of lessons
in the school of love—but most of all a mutual agreement to
continue in the relationship, by, with, and for each other. It is in
this area of commitment to each other that an intimate relationship between a man and a woman has its turning point—and
there are as many failures as successes. The paradox of separateness and unity is one that must be worked out differently in
each case, with no easy answers or simple rules that always
work.

Diogenes Allen has written in his book *Love*: "The union or
oneness that Christianity endorses in romantic love and
marriage is that of a common or *shared life*. Two people in
marriage remain distinct individuals. They are not to try to become one by absorbing each other, but to respect the irreducible
'otherness' of each person in their love....Romantic love can
achieve this unique and delicate relation in marriage only if each
person can recognize, respect, and cherish the independent reality of the other."

Identifying what is meant, in particular, by "independent reality" is not always easy. My paternal grandparents had a kind
of love and commitment that looked most of the time like two
separate lives. As far back as I can remember, my grandfather,
who had heart trouble, was retired and stayed around the house
all of the time. He loved to tend his backyard garden, fix little
things around the house, and make small useful or decorative
objects in his workshop in the basement—such as tiny wooden
doll chairs I still cherish. My grandmother I remember as practically living in her kitchen, always tending to something that was
boiling on the burners. She talked more than he did, usually
gently complaining about the "old man" being around, doing
nothing, and all the work *she* had to do, while he "fiddled
around"—but all with a definite twinkle in her eyes.

I believe they loved each other deeply in a way that was enjoyed but not spoken of by them or their five sons. They held together a household through the Depression, two wars, illnesses

and crushing financial setbacks. And it was a home everyone wanted to return to—there was no question where the center of love was on Henderson Street.

While I was growing up, their marriage was never my ideal of love; I was too young to understand. But now I come closer to appreciating what I can recognize as a deep, everyday commitment that stood the test of time. When I think of such relationships as are possible between men and women, I see their style of coping and enduring as only one possibility. Such is the richness of texture possible between two very different people, which can bring order and design to life as mere sameness cannot. Someone has likened the music of marriage to the possibility of hitting a full range of notes on a keyboard rather than sticking to the center handspan, or playing only white or only black notes, as some of my early piano-learning songs required for novelty.

The risks and the potential benefits of men and women friendships are many, so it is no wonder that building such complexity of relationship takes some working up to in our own personal growth. As children we tended to stick to friends of our own sex for any close relationships—apart from the tomboy, or the boy who was left with only girl cousins to play with on vacations. This same-sex affinity seems to be less true today as children go to preschools earlier and learn a variety of roles. Now little boys wear aprons to gather dirty dishes and help wash them up, while girls are known to collect toy cars and think about careers before the first grade.

Children who are friends with the opposite sex early in life have many advantages, and whatever mystery is lost is well replaced by healthy reality. Boy-girl friendships seem an important preparation for the otherness of men or women that children will encounter all along the way up through their adult lives. Someone who is part of our everyday world is also a potential friend.

When children become adolescents (which also seems to occur earlier and earlier in succeeding generations) they usually begin to experience some of the pull, the attraction toward the opposite sex that is a foretaste of what a later union could be. These are times of learning how to distinguish the reality of love from the illusion, discerning the limits of togetherness and the meaning of separateness—and growing in those lessons as quickly and as well as possible, before more serious commitments are made, and before the results are too lasting.

Then there is a period (perhaps it never ends) of defining ourselves as adult women or men, an enrichment process to enable fuller and more satisfying revelation of the self to another in friendship, in marriage.

The particular emotion and joy of consummation in Plato's myth is an appealing but dangerous paradigm of why people often seek their opposite in a relationship, and especially in marriage. We are perhaps never more tempted to merge our separate selves—to sacrifice our individuality for the sake of unity, for the comforts and securities of having that one person who is with us and for us for a lifetime—than we are in marriage.

There is no doubt that the myth is based on a reality in which people seek to complete something within themselves, and feel in a romantic surge that this would be possible through a merging with one's opposite, so that the two form a whole. This intense experience, this desire and belief that such a "completion" is possible, is called "projection." However, rather than serving as a path to unity and wholeness, it can also be an attempt to avoid working on those hidden, "shadow" aspects of our own souls, which we do not recognize as yet, or do not wish to face and deal with in our own personalities. Thus we attribute them to other people, or to one other person.

In Charles Williams's superb novel *Descent into Hell*, an elderly professor's obsession with a young woman, Adela, reaches the point at which he must conjure up a phantom woman to fulfill his need of her, with no regard for her otherness and her separate personal reality:

"It was Adela, yet it was not. It was her height and had her movement. The likeness appeased him, yet he did not understand the faint unlikeness....He knew it could not be Adela, for even Adela had never been so like Adela as this. That truth which is the vision of romantic love, in which the beloved becomes supremely her own adorable and external self, the glory and splendor of her own existence, and her own existence no longer felt or thought as hers but of and from another, that was aped for him then."

As John A. Sanford writes:

"To the extent that a relationship is founded on projection, the element of human love is lacking. To be in love with someone we do not know as a person, but are attracted to because they reflect back to us the god or goddess in our souls, is, in a sense to be in love with oneself, not with the other person....To be capable of real love means becoming mature, with realistic expectations of the other person....This is not to say that projection is a bad thing....Each time projection occurs there is another opportunity of...knowing our own souls." He points out realistically that projection is most often the factor that initially draws the sexes together, and that since men and women are so unlike, it takes quite a powerful force to bring them together at all.

But the question is always *What happens next?* In the friendships that occur either in or out of marriage, this is the cross—this is the crossroads. And the decisions that are made affect all of one's life from that point on in the story. Do the partners separate with honor? Or, as friends, do they begin to discover and enjoy the actual reality of each other's day-to-day lives?

In the context of Christian marriage, when committed partners begin to discover the fallenness, the ordinariness, the flaws of the human being (not the god or goddess) they have married, can they live in the imperfect context of good human companionship and mutual choices for improvement? When she turns out to be a procrastinator and tasks are left undone; when his ambition throws their love out of focus; when children complicate the scene—*what happens next?* Are they willing to learn to live with the reality of the person they have happily and unhappily married, and give unselfishly to the other to make the reality better?

Can they begin to see that the school of love is also most clearly and importantly the way of forgiveness, of forgiving the one who sins against us, aware and unaware; as that person also chooses to forgive us, again and again, because this is Christ's way?

And is there some semblance of equality in the relationship on a deep level—that of the spiritual worth of two different, worthy souls? Marriage should not be a scenario for developing either martyrs or heroes.

All the lessons we have learned from other friendships, of mutual choices, in learning to agree, focusing on another's good, sharing ourselves in love and laughter, stretching our interests for the sake of the beloved, being there with, by, and for another—should come into play in marriage. But the very fact of being male and female, and thus often quite opposite, is always a factor, and often it is the crux of the cross.

What we hope for is the completion of the beautiful myth of conjunction of halves that have been ingloriously separated for a period of exile and now are happily united (the story line of every love movie or fairy tale)—a happy state of continuance that rarely occurs with the satisfaction and permanence we would like to celebrate.

Instead, we find in relationships between men and women all levels of attractions, projections that can result in friendship, grow into marriage, remain outside marriage, survive the marriage of each to another person, or die at any point. There are choices to be made, clearly, whenever any attraction occurs; friendship is as legitimate a choice to make as marriage. A chaste friendship as an affirmation of love is right for some; more usually, marriage ensues.

Unity can also occur between men and women outside of marriage in relationships that retain something of the beauty and glory of opposites finding each other, without the ongoing experience of shared common life. One of my favorite examples of this joining of personalities is the friendship of St. Francis and his friend Clare, his disciple and fellow servant of God. "Those who observed Clare and Francis with purely human eyes would think they walked separately the road to God," writes Murray Bodo in *The Francis Book*, "that they were distant and removed from each other. But if they had eyes of the spirit, they would see two hearts inseparably joined, two souls united in God."

One story is told of the intensity of the flame of friendship between these two: Clare once had a great desire to eat a meal with her friend when he stayed in Assisi, but he always refused to bestow on her that favor. Finally he was persuaded by his companions to grant her desire. Plans were made to hold the meal at the church where she had taken her own religious vows. When they sat down to eat, along with their companions, grouped around that humble table, "Francis began to speak about God in such a sweet and holy and profound and divine and marvelous way that he himself and Saint Clare and her companion and all the others who were at that poor little table were rapt in God by the overabundance of divine grace that descended upon them....It seemed to the men of Assisi and Bettona and the entire district that the Church of Saint Mary of the Angels and the whole place and the forest...were all aflame, and that an immense fire was burning over all of them.

"But when they reached the place, they saw that nothing was on fire....Then they knew for sure that it had been a heavenly and not a material fire that God had miraculously shown them to symbolize the fire of divine love." So they withdrew, with great consolation; and after a long while Francis and Clare "came back to themselves" refreshed by spiritual as well as physical food.

This beautiful, simple scenario of the intensity and power found in a friendship of opposites, both dedicated to God, infused with his Spirit, is a paradigm of any friendship of great commitment, where the gifts brought by the two are nearly a perfect fit, forming a sphere of purity and dedication, a conflagration of good.

But seeking some quality we lack in a member of the opposite sex, apart from real charity, maturity, and realistic commitment, is not always fruitful. While the feeling of incompleteness can be a compelling force toward joining up with another person, it can also become an excuse for avoiding another kind of development: finding, acknowledging, and nurturing qualities that your true self longs for *in yourself.* Marriage, friendship of a deep devotion, can seem to be a shortcut to filling in those spaces in the soul. But in reality there are few such shortcuts in life.

Truly less is risked in friendship, or in early romance, with one who embodies the completion of our soul—either the female soul or component in a man's personality ("anima"); or the male soul or component in a woman's personality ("animus"). Too much weight put upon the ideal, with too little emphasis on the reality of the relationship may lead us into hero worship or slavish devotion rather than the humble meal that marriage more nearly represents through life.

Perhaps one reason this experience of projection is so common, and we follow its call so blindly, is that we are unable even to see that it is the completion of our own self we are seeking. Our desire is not simply for romantic love, as appealing as that can be, but for something beyond, something God longs for us to have. In our need for each other, we participate unaware in God's longing for us.

"I love you for yourself," and "I love you for what I am when I am with you," are not necessarily opposites, but they are not the same either. The first, when initially uttered, is perhaps never fully true; though if it is a desire and a goal to discover and live responsibly with the true "other" you will discover, it is not a lie. The second is perhaps too much a focus on the self if it predominates. Yet it too can be part of a committed love, if the friend is never merely an object for our own self-improvement. Both insights are true; but the opportunity for delusion is great. It is not necessary that our friendship be totally altruistic, for then it is not mutuality, but charity—in the limited sense of helping out someone weaker or dependent on our love and care.

Robertson Davies writes through the wise eyes of a Jungian analyst in his novel *The Manticore*, that "the Anima must look like somebody. You projected...the Anima on their perfectly ordinary heads. But you can never see the Anima pure and simple, because she has no such existence; you will always see her in terms of something or someone else." The same is true of the animus. We must get at these truths in particular ways within the scope of our individual lives. As part of the process, those early associations we may have had of superhuman figures with the beloved become gradually less important (or should, in a healthy relationship) than a fulfilling day-to-day love.

The result can be cruel if such a sea change does not occur, if both members of a couple do not grow up—growing both within themselves and toward acceptance of their particular life situation. For both men and women act unkindly toward or become indifferent to those they feel have enchanted or waylaid them. A wise person will want the human dimension of the relationship acknowledged and accepted from the beginning, even somehow in the haze of romantic bliss. The beloved's flaws and inconsistencies are all a part of life; how he or she adjusts to reality is a better indication of character than the projections of each other one may cherish from courtship.

Rather, as the relationship grows, perhaps we will be able to learn, simultaneously, how deficient is the love that we thought we brought to the other; yet how full of grace is the opportunity to grow into whatever unity is possible in *this* situation. In the process, our own limitations, which were the initial reason for seeking out the other, become less a gaping need than an opportunity to truly value what is outside the self. And often as a bonus, in the process, what we sincerely love can gradually, naturally become a part of our own personality. This is the sea change in the view of the other and the self that must occur if a friendship, especially between man and woman, is to mature, or even to endure.

How does such a change occur? Usually it is not possible except through pain, through suffering with and even for the other, not as the giving and taking of abuse (too often the scenario, in which victim and hero find each other and act out the drama of archetypes to its tragic end). But as a kind of seesaw in which one is willing to be "down" temporarily for the other, knowing that when life rocks the other way, the friend who is mate will also hold the other aloft. It only works in the actual up and down motion of a life, when neither loses faith in the process.

It is a great risk to agree to be there, for and with someone into the murky future, for we cannot choose our hardships, all of our tasks, or put a limit on what love will be called upon to endure. We may both be forced into straits when there is no one to hold us securely, in strength. But in the friendship that is Christian marriage, love is to be built on something besides the other's achievement, or on the degree to which the person fulfills us, or on martyr-like self-sacrifice. God is in the friendship too, suffering, guiding, and showing that there is a way to live.

Christ the friend gives yet another dimension to the precarious experience of male/female bonding in love. Some have called him the third Person in the partnership. His presence by and with and for us as individuals ought to be part of the mix, the acceptance always of grace, so that the spiritual good of the other is preeminent. Thus the question of what it will cost us is less important than what God will teach us through our particular experience of love. Did not the cross cost Christ all?

In any friendship, the questions all come back to the self.

Am I here only for myself or somehow mysteriously also for others? To what extent am I able to love (and willing to learn to increase in love) beyond myself and my good?

Marriage is one avenue of fulfillment. Yet the "oughts" and "shoulds" of marriage can at various times either stifle or perpetuate the friendship that is possible, but not easily attainable, between men and women. Sometimes we are led to renunciation of the early vision of attraction. In Davies' *The Manticore* one character speaks of such a renunciation:

"The women we really love are the women who complete us; who have the qualities we can borrow and so become something nearer to whole men. Just as we complete them, of course...when romance was stripped away, we were too much alike; our strengths and weaknesses were too nearly the same. Together we would have doubled our gains and our losses, but that isn't what love is."

Friendship in marriage, a love of something outside the self, can offer great hope. Man-woman attractions as a way of discovering and accepting our own souls can lead us full circle through romantic love and friendship, back to what Davies calls a "rebirth," completing our own sphere of personhood, at once denying and embracing the myth of "one soul in two bodies."

As Charles Williams writes of the poet Dante's experience of encountering Beatrice: "He says that when she met him in the street and said good-morning, he was so highly moved that he was, for the moment, in a state of complete good-will, complete *caritas* toward everyone. 'I have been,' he said...after that description, 'at that point of life beyond which he who passes cannot return.'...It is a region from which no creature returns afterwards. One is never the same again."

LOOKING AT FRIENDSHIP

1. What qualities have we most admired in friends we have had of the opposite sex? Have we increasingly learned to develop those qualities in ourselves through our associations with those very real people in our lives?

> The degree to which I can create relationships which facilitate the growth of others as separate persons is a measure of the growth I have achieved in myself—Carl R. Rogers.

2. What do I do with the lessons about myself I have learned through failures in man-woman friendships, on any level? How can these lessons be brought in a healing way into the story of my relationship with God?

CHAPTER EIGHT

Parents and Children: A New Shape of Friendship

Parenthood is an ongoing apprenticeship in the school of love for both parent and child. It is almost a new language of love, although it bears some resemblance to the tongue you spoke earlier, with other people. There is some transfer of meaning, and some of the rules and expectations are similar. But speaking it sounds and feels quite differently on the tongue.

For me it is a new shape of love, only hinted at in other cases, but never felt with such intensity and never so filled with paradox. For friendship between a parent and child carries with it an inequality between oneself and the child that must be worked out, gradually, in love, until the little one can be rediscovered in more of an equality of friendship, of full personality and responsibility, later in life.

Perhaps nothing tests our innate need to control others, to make reality conform to our image, more than the experience of a child who invades our world and remakes it and us, in the most innocent of ways—simply by being. As I wrote of my second-born:

> Where did this one come from?
>   Bone of my bone
> and other as the back of the sun.
>
> She takes up space that isn't there to be taken
>   Somehow makes it her own.
>
> Keep me humble/no problem that.
>
> How to mother a star intact in its own sky
> Or a slice of the rainbow the hand passes through?

Firm and wiggly on my knee
　As to-be-reckoned-with as the morning
And slippery as quicksilver.

Did you choose me or I you?
Nevermind.

Love in a new form, you are exactly as you
　are.

Deo gratias.

Simply to reach out and hold, to discover daily just the shape
and sound and demands of a totally new person somehow
bequeathed to your care, yet never truly *yours*, starts us on a
path of increasing knowledge. And always in those steps we encounter both joy and pain, often so intermingled that to even try
to sort out the difference would break us and incapacitate our
love in the moment. Instead, in the friendship of parent and
child, our natural longing for mutual wholeness comes to the
fore, while perfectionism and its demons must constantly, of necessity, be pushed aside. For to require another to conform to
our idea of being, to seek to control another in order to fulfill
some need in ourselves, is subtly to destroy.

In reality, here is a new piece of creation—on our knee, in our
sphere. And we are called to love in the particularity of our constantly changing, often unpredictable circumstances—surely the
most difficult arena of all. For what a child demands of us is our
very being—with and by and for her, in the unrepeatable moment. Such love is hardly ever convenient or easy—or unre-
warded, I have found, when it is embraced on its own terms: in
the smile of acceptance, the gentleness of forgiveness, and the
spoken or unspoken promise of ongoing love.

It is said that the opposite of love is not hate, but indifference.
And the love a parent is called upon to give a child is surely the
kind of love that cares intimately, that desires a conjunction of
wills with the child, but will not (modeling itself after God's
love) coerce love, desiring it to be returned freely.

So much of our children's path in the early years is perilous,
during which we are guardians of their well-being, especially in
early growth, and well into their school years. We are there as
friends to keep them from harm, to preserve their very lives, to

show them by our example what life is like, and, even more, what it can yet be through love. We struggle to delineate the shape of it, to cast light on the variations of experience we ourselves wrestle with daily.

I feel now that I was brought up to be too fearful of life—of impending disasters such as potential accidents, dangerous people, and "risky" activities; I was even discouraged from going to summer camp with all its perils. Thus I never had experiences which my own, more viable children today take for granted. I decided early that I didn't want them to experience such restrictions on what was possible for them, and that even if takes concentrated prayer and letting go as I send them off, it is better than their growing up too limited and unsure of themselves. I had to find my own daredevil experiences much later—in more dangerous ways, to compensate. And yet my parents' prayers for me also saw me miraculously through.

Yet often, I wish my children had just a bit more *realistic* fear of some of the possibilities of danger. They are, compared to me, utterly fearless and indefatigable. Their attitudes are part of the changing shape of love, generation to generation, to which we all must continually adjust.

Knowing and being a friend to my children is almost a new geometry, a new understanding of shapes and spatial relationships, never an easy subject for me to grasp. Once again I am back to basics in the school of love, and the tasks and demands stretch my patience and my imagination in unaccustomed ways. In this new geometry we adopt a new angle from which to look at relationships. From this vantage point we view some of the perils and obstacles to learning the steps of love while another small one walks beside us. Our child is at once intimately related to us, and undeniably separate from us—another soul somehow in our temporary care, forever changing the lines of our own destiny.

"Love proceeds either from nature, or from duty..." writes Aelred, "from nature, as a mother loves her child; from duty, through giving and receiving." These two strands of love, the given, maternal feeling and instinctive wisdom of the body that carries us through early stages of the labyrinth; and the intelligence of duty, applied here and now, together serve to build up the shape of love, parent to child.

Last year when I was part-time director of adult education at our church, my daughters were finally both enrolled in preschool classes, and I had mornings free to be in my office, go to staff meetings, and make contacts in the community. The knowledge that they were happily involved with children their own age, and well taken care of, enabled me to work unhindered, uninterrupted. I was just returning to a job after being home with the children full-time, and I was attempting the juggling act of career and family that women seem to find practically unavoidable, trying to meet conflicting needs with grace and a sense of equilibrium. Some days worked beautifully, and other days were a disaster.

We are always tested most in the specifics, not in ideal scenarios. How are we to be with, by, and for another—a friend in the moment? We do our best, out of duty and necessity, and an underlying sense of the privilege of expressing what we can convey of love on the way.

For example, in my work I value efficiency and speed, while my children love to dawdle and experiment with all the tangible opportunities of a trip or task. Conflict arises between us, sometimes at every step, challenging my love, stretching me. Thus the line of duty, of love, is never a completely straight seam, connecting two points. This is the new geometry I am being taught.

Sometimes, when the children had minor illnesses or the schools had holidays, I ended up taking one or the other of the girls to work with me, to sit and color on the floor of my office, or to pull wildly at books in the bookcases, beg for paper and crayons, and always to plead for more attention than I could give from my desk. I tried somehow to work around their much-loved but distracting, dividing presence.

On one occasion I brought my two-year-old to walk along with me to put up posters in various parts of the large church plant. She insisted on carrying one of the colorful cardboard sheets, larger than herself, dragging it as we made our slow descent down to a lower level. As Emilie and I wandered through the church building, stopping on the steps to tie a shoe, to look out the window at other children playing outdoors, to catch and savor every detail of the experience, to pick up the inevitably falling poster, I found myself impatient and my purposes strained. These are the times of sudden shock and reevaluation of the things we thought we already knew. Have the rules changed? Have I?

What is life, in the school of love? Is it primarily a destination we need to reach, in X number of minutes, by the least circuitous route? There are duties to employers, to ourselves, to our dependents. All of these are real and important. But there is also a call to let go, to "let God," to relax in the impossibilities as well as the certainties, and thereby to see accomplished what duty alone could never perform.

Children know, and teach us, that the journey is all, the steps we take in life that eventually get us from here to there. My sense of shape and self, through these years of parent-child friendship, has been challenged, my mind stretched by accommodating myself to another's presence. We are there by, with, and for our child; and the child cannot reciprocate equally. Her gifts are hidden, her very presence releasing them gradually, as I can comprehend and accept. This too is a grace of friendship.

Friendship with children is at times a very physical task. My adult body, used to speed and an economy of action, felt (then quite intensely, now less so) unequally yoked to my child's fully alive and curious body, with arms and legs that determine their own space and flail to demand more room. Two-year-olds haven't learned the rules of politeness that keep us from touching, from playing when we're expected to be accomplishing something, and they unwittingly create new configurations of demand, complexities of relationship by their presence.

For instance, the lines and patterns of modern family life are persistent challenges to our individual shapes and to our identity in love. So many of our lessons are, of necessity, a solitary experience, though we are connected too. At the time of these struggles, the girls' father was traveling on business frequently, and the square symmetry of our family would become, for a week or more, a triangle of one parent and two children. Lessons would have to be learned and unlearned; figures drawn and erased as though on a chalkboard, leaving indistinct traces behind.

Furthermore, I would feel pulled in two opposite directions by both children, a struggle that challenged the shape of my love in another way, as I tried to fulfill the sometimes conflicting demands of parenting these two very different girls. For instance, one child is most decisive and stubborn once she has made her choice, whether it is the color of a lollipop or an attitude to adopt; the other prefers to keep her options open as long as possible and prolong the delicious process of choosing—until we're all ready to force her hand, make her choice for her, and drag her away!

It was humbling for me to learn to deal in the basics again, just as my children were also learning the basic shapes of circle, square, and triangle. Sometimes in love, in friendship, we think we have reached a plateau: "I've got it!" And just then, we trip on the step, fumble the play, and fall flat on our faces.

Fortunately, one stage prepares us for another in the mysterious pattern of children's growth and increasing independence. I remember the earlier geometry of holding an infant in my arms, that sense of unity on a feeling level that says simply that love is a circle of protection and nurture, surely a sign of heaven. And then, gradually, a mother experiences a necessary pulling apart from that closeness as she and the child become two separate spheres of activity, mother and toddler, with ever new signs and lessons to learn.

Recognizing lines, learning a new shape, and connecting the dots of an invisible picture in a puzzle book are activities a growing child develops in tandem. But I am learning that parents need to learn such basics on another level—to see how the lines of their lives are connected by love, waiting to be drawn by us, the pattern underlying the page, open to the eye of imagination and risk. We need to see these lines as connecting but not constricting, flexible enough to accommodate the new lessons, yet tautly secure when safety and strength are required to hold us in love.

Walking along with a child, on interrupted steps, I swallow hard often and resign myself to her pace and allowing her distractions along the way. But I know in my heart that the reason to rush to my frenzied, singleminded goals has vanished in the spirit of this new love, this new shape of friendship she offers.

Polly Berrien Berends writes in *Whole Child, Whole Parent*: "The parent is like a conductor of an orchestra. The conductor is not a powerful person. It appears so. On the surface it seems that the music is produced by the power of the conductor to tell everyone what to do and when to do it. He may have to do that, but it is not what makes the music. A good conductor does not merely tell everyone what to do; rather he helps everyone to *hear what is so*. For this he is not primarily a telling but a listening individual: even while the orchestra is performing loudly he is listening inwardly to silent music. He is not so much commanding as he is obedient."

It would be easy to miss (as I sometimes lost my grasp on) the richness of these times, this experience of obedience—learning together how to make the shape of our lives fit each other, to grow into a configuration of parent-child friendship, which is always a custom design.

The Psalmist says that "the boundary lines have fallen for me in pleasant places" (Ps. 16:6), and these boundaries may refer to the territory of a promised land, the limits of a person, the restrictions of a situation—or all of the above. For me it is a prayer I walk in as I precariously learn my way of conducting, how to limn my personal lines as friend, as parent.

Learning this lesson, developing the capacity to know our boundaries and to *bless* them, is the ongoing work of a lifetime. To acknowledge and accept limits is to be able to focus on the task itself. Perhaps it is hardest as we learn practical friendship in our own families, the significant adjustments, as our lines of individual differentiation come up against each other's needs daily in a challenge to being who we are, by and for each other.

In recent years the shape of my life has changed from office worker to stay-at-home mother to part-time worker with small children. The shape of friendship with my children changes along with these important adjustments. The outer lines have an effect on my soul as well. Jobs can be taken, arrangements made, but our inner life struggles to keep pace with the outer delineations of duty and affection, of needs and problems.

The prophet Isaiah, who writes of God sitting "enthroned above the circle of the earth," commands, "Lift your eyes and look to the heavens: Who created all these?" (40:22, 26). The school of love is a picture lesson in shapes and colors, from the glories of our round earth, the lines of sunlight and shadow, the shapes of sun and moon, all of creation doing God's will—to our own lines and shapes and positions in this drama.

I will always be asking "What is required here and now?" The most important lesson on the journey is to *see* what is really there. I must first observe, recognize differences and demands, make comparisons, and step out in risk, in love.

"The eye is the lamp of the body. So, if your eye is sound, your whole body will be full of light" (Matt. 6:22). In the stretching of my soul and its boundaries to include friendship and duty, my children continue to teach me a lesson I first learned when visiting cathedrals: "Don't forget to look up." Do not miss all of the beauty of this walk; *look up,* as well as down at the path ahead, to prevent stumbling. Don't forsake what you have to do, but keep your eyes also on the glory. One builds discipline; the other is to engender hope.

It is I who am usually in danger of missing the beauty, the gifts of an unhurried walk or an interrupted task, not to see it as the texture of the more-important lessons of love and friendship along the way. The hopes and dreams of our friendship, parent and child, are like circles above us—bright balloons that we hold tenuously—inviting, precarious, seeming to slip through our fingers as their elevations shift and change.

One parent tells of her young children's experience of toy hot air balloons. The children, impatient and in awe, would always let go of the expensive playthings too soon, just to watch them go. The parents lamented the waste of money, but the children loved the sight of the colored circles receding from them in flight. In later years the children learned to hold on a bit longer and more tightly, while the parents increasingly found they could let go of prudence and enjoy the freedom of flight themselves.

These are the tasks of friendship in parenthood, the holding on and the letting go; knowing which to do when; how tightly and how long. Our lives together are gifts to us, somehow held in God's hand, revealed in love, as we are able to bear the truth, in these recurring patterns and shapes of love, of friendship.

LOOKING AT FRIENDSHIP

1. Draw a picture that shows the shape of yourself and those you love, and how the shapes relate to each other. What is

your personal geometry, what are the demands of duty and of love, in these friendships?

> When a child loves you for a long, long time, not just to play with, but really loves you, then you become real—Margery Wilson.

2. What are the lessons of holding on in your life today? What are the lessons of letting go? How can they fit together, as parts of the paradox of friendship with that one you love?

CHAPTER NINE

When Friendship Falters

T he time and place from which to examine the failure of friendship—that flaw in the story, the broken tie, the dissonant chord—is when we can be surrounded by true friends, pillars of strength, around us. When we are held, supported by others who have shared our story to this point, we may be able to look at our loss in perspective.

I have had several friends—a handful, perhaps—on whom I can no longer count to be there, with and for me. And perhaps they have now become my sharpest critics, if not active enemies. Those who know us best, who have shared our table and our thoughts in intimate circumstances, also have the most with which to wound us should friendship turn to enmity.

The causes for faltering friendship are many and varied. With one friend, I simply moved away and someone else became her confidante—someone with whom I did not feel comfortable. Communication with my friend became strained—then broken. In another case, a competitive spirit grew up between us. Perhaps it was not entirely our fault, but circumstances separated us until retrieval seemed impossible. Finally we would have felt almost traitors had we returned to our former closeness, due to new and incompatible professional loyalties.

True friendship is the extension of ourselves to touch another, perhaps to allow that one passage into territory we ourselves have never explored. To offer one's heart is an exercise of great vulnerability and risk, but it is also part of being alive, of being fully human. Thus it is disturbing to admit what the Psalmist laments in Psalm 55: that painful separations do occur, even after levels of trust seem to have been rewarded, and even when the context of the friendship was once that of trust and a shared life in the context of community. The Psalmist mourns the end of friendship:

> Had it been an adversary...then I could have
> borne it;
>> or had it been an enemy who vaunted himself
>> against me, then I could have hidden from him.
> But it was you, one after my own heart,
>> my companion, my own familiar friend.
> We took sweet counsel together,
>> and walked with the throng in the house of God
> —Psalm 55:12-14.

Such friendship has enormously high stakes. It should not be broken irretrievably—I wish I could say that it *cannot*. How can love be separated from itself? Someone has written: "Love you? I *am* you." Aelred writes that: "When friendship has made of two one, just as that which is one cannot be divided, so also friendship cannot be separated from itself. Therefore it is evident that a friendship which permits of division, was never...true."

In the words of St. Jerome, *"Friendship which can end, was never true friendship."* Yet we are not always sure, in the sudden breach of relationship, whether what we are dealing with is a flaw that existed in the design of the friendship from the beginning, or a true break in what once was authentic and strong. In any friendship there might be a time for pulling back, to escape the intensity of being there for another; it may look like the negation of love. Friendships can also alter when one moves away, another takes on new familial responsibilities...a friend becomes ill, starts a new job, or becomes engrossed in a time-consuming hobby or project—many changes can be accommodated and allowed for within friendship.

Ties can be relaxed, rather than broken; privileges and duties may be altered or foregone for the time being. But if the respect and love for the person and for oneself endures, then it cannot be truly said that a friendship has died under those new conditions. A break in rhythm, a spell of silence, a breather from the intensity of coordinate lives, all may be part of the story of friendship.

We use reason as well as our hearts to seek the truth, to try to understand what is the true situation. And in this there are guidelines to help us brave such fierce waters.

Aelred says, "Listen, then, not to my words, but to Scripture: 'Although he has drawn a sword at a friend, despair not; for there may be a returning to a friend. If he opens a sad mouth, fear not.' Consider what this means. If your friend...for a time withdraws himself from you, if sometimes he prefers his own counsel to yours, if he disagrees with you in any opinion or discussion, do not think your friendship must be dissolved because of these differences."

In many modern friendships we may encounter some of the same obstacles as I have found to separate me from those I once perceived to be my friends. Ronald A. Sharp writes in *Friendship and Literature*: "To claim that friendship often involves competition, aggression, and self-interest does not discredit friendship; it merely states the obvious. The important questions are how friends find ways of protecting themselves against these liabilities and how, in some cases, they transform them into assets."

I have seen this positive experience as well. It was hard to understand the fierce competitiveness of one writer friend of mine, who seemed not to notice others' feelings in seeking to further advance a rocketing career with new publishing contracts and sought-after fame. But I have come closer to accepting this person's aggressiveness as a component of personality and individual drive, as I have myself encountered more hardship and a need to stand up for myself in a highly competitive field in recent years. I do not feel so harshly toward this friend now, and many new avenues within our friendship have become possible.

Yet sometimes we never come around to understanding another's way of being with us. Sometimes friendship does falter and fail. Or what we thought was a cord of unbreakable connection, soul to soul, was not so. The shock of such a discovery is felt through our entire being, for it affects our sense of ourselves and what the friend had contributed to that understanding; it may cause us to doubt our own judgment and hinder future intimacy with others, for fear of greater loss; even our trust in God's goodness in the gift of friendship can become strained.

I am not one who is quick to mark *canceled* on any relationship. For it is doubly difficult to rebuild after a break if both people have hardened their hearts. Somehow, I want to believe in the power of the truth, of the strength of love extended at least one way along the cord of connection, that is able to reactivate the bond, enliven the fire with even the smallest spark of life.

I always instinctively want to give the benefit of the doubt, if that is the balm that is needed to get through the crisis in a friendship. Generally I have found that in smaller breaches of connection, it is possible to find reconciliation. Friendship will soon reestablish itself when both people agree as to what truly happened and decide how to mend it reciprocally and speedily.

But in larger breaks, the suspicion of disloyalty, of jealousy that colors good will, I have found that such suspension of judgment is not the answer. Despite what seem to me to be good intentions, I must admit to failure, because one person alone cannot bring about intimacy. Sometimes there are facts underlying the relationship that simply war against connection, against unity. It takes great moral courage to be willing to uncover the truth, even though it may cost us the loss of one we hold dear. Pascal writes of such friendships that "we should seek the truth without hesitation; and, if we refuse it, we show that we value the esteem of men more than the search for truth."

For me, facing facts is often even harder than waiting and hoping, squarely admitting that what had seemed to be a bond of strength was based on something else: projection, which occurs not only between the sexes, but also among members of the same sex; selfishness; the hope of personal gain through association with another.

How can we tell whether what we feel is true admiration that is capable of blossoming into love and friendship or a lesser attraction? Someone once said of the poet/novelist Charles Williams, "He found the gold in all of us and made it shine." That quality of bringing out the best of what is already in another is a true gift of friendship. Would that each of us could do this for others!

But we do not always see so clearly, in the attraction and interchange among people we meet, when their gifts are offered to us, what may underlie their motives—or our own. These truths are stumbled upon hard, and heavily, when they must be faced, in the loss of one who was once dear to us. Often I have been the one who must reluctantly admit that the moment has passed to revive a dead friendship, and that my wish not to lose anyone, and most especially not *this* one, at *this* time, is unrealistic.

Such a moment can be compared to a painting in which two people stand together; the gaze of one person acknowledges joy in the presence of the other, and the arms, if not touching, reach out. But the gaze of the other is steady and outward, the stance more detached, suggesting imminent movement away from the friend. It is a subtle study in two wills that no longer are bridged—but only one person knows that there has been a change. While the friend trusts and accommodates, the companion has begun to look elsewhere. It is a picture of abandonment, of pain. The absence is doubly painful because of the high stakes, the level of commitment within the fellowship of believers.

Life both changes and needs change—and our friends are as human and flawed as we are. "Love, like fire, can only exist in eternal movement, and love ceases to live as soon as it ceases hoping and fearing," wrote La Rochefoucauld. The cords, then, are more like fire than twine, full of air and passion, so that friends can be cut off by internal changes in one or both partners, invisible to see, yet real as flame.

I have written letters that have assumed a mutual love and remembrance; they must have fallen into a black hole rather than a mailbox, for all I ever received back. Silence, absence, lack of response (how long does a friend wait, or hope—or fear?) are signs, as sure as anger and abuse, that friendship has faltered along the way.

If the opposite of love is not hate but indifference, then many friendships die somewhere in their early stages of growth and watering for this neglect. The moment when friends say to each other, "You, too? I thought I was the only one?"—the magic of connecting, palm to palm, spirit to spirit, holds also within it the potential for the breaking of that invisible cord of flame that is love so bravely extended.

But not everyone has that vision, or can wait. The grass looks greener, even absence and loss are compelling. The moment comes when one friend discloses, "I am hurt," or "This is very important to me." The response is silence, indifference, or even disdain.

Friendship can falter at any stage for lack of watering or nurturing, for neglecting to truly listen to the other. It can range from cutting off a potential act of caring, refusing to meet, in kind, an extension of the other's hopes and fears—to encompass a wide range of betrayal and abuse of confidences. My friend Carol says that she knew her relationship with her oldest college friend was no longer what it had been when she heard what Sally was saying about her, rumors she had passed on without going to Carol first. After that, anything Carol wanted to say to her friend sounded defensive, and a fragile trust was broken.

Friendship can also falter from lack of information, or from too much information that is misused, misapplied in regard to the other. Friendship means that when doubt exists, we look first to our friend and do not trust another source in order to find out the truth. It takes trust on both sides not to deceive and to tell what is appropriate; to disclose oneself honestly and sensitively within the relationship for the purpose of each other's good.

Learning how to tell when our friend has looked away, begun to pull out of the picture, is a precarious but necessary lesson. Some people err on the side of jumping to conclusions based on too little information. Some may hope, as I have, for too long that they have not read the signals properly, that there is some new factor that will reveal itself and bring the picture back into focus. Sometimes this can be self-deception.

Yet, with some friendships, thankfully, such grace has occurred. After an absence, even after years apart, a friend and I find we have both grown, and in the same direction, under very different circumstances. Pamela is such a friend; I count her among my most precious companions. Our friendship is like a gem saved from rubble, one we treasure in ongoing relationship.

If we think we can "control" friendship—whom we choose to be called on to love, how we will respond when we are tested, and the exact course of the relationship—we fool ourselves. And we overestimate the power of our own love to hold things together. This can be a costly lesson. Friendship—like marriage—is, in Madeleine L'Engle's phrase, a "two-part invention." When one voice becomes fainter, then appears absent, usually there is no friendship. There may be a shell, a pretense, for a time, before the true situation is revealed. In this period of transition, false hope may be as damaging as hasty judgment.

How do we cope, and how do we live in the gap between friendship and loss, between knowing and not-knowing?

In friendship that falters somewhere along the way, we are looking at the question of appearance versus reality. All of my own experiences of loss have entailed this crucible, the unavoidable crossroads of coming to grips with *what is really there* as opposed to what people are saying, or even doing, that may look like "love."

And what will I do in the face of this loss of love?

I have not yet fully learned detachment, that being/action of the saints in which all that matters is God, and we are, in the best sense, unmoved by the chances and changes of fortunes and friendship, life and death.

"'Detachment' consists, not in casting aside all natural loves and goods, but in the possession of a love and a good so great that all others, though they may and do acquire increase through the presence of the greater love and good, which explains and justifies them, seem nothing in comparison," writes Coventry Patmore in *The Rod, the Root and the Flower.*

These very real breaks in friendship do not seem "nothing" to me. I am wounded and ache for the losses I have sustained, especially when I do not understand how and when love turned, and why this much loss must be sustained on earth. The question one always asks is, "When did this change?" How could I have missed the clues; the glancing aside, the moving away, the withdrawal of empathy and identification, the absence of "taking one's part"? Yet even in the face of these questions, God's love is the central pillar of strength, and those who are faithful around us enhance that support.

But any loss seems to weaken the structure of the city, produces cracks in our edifice, seems to leave us less than we were. No one else can ever exactly take another's place, make up for a specific absence. This is a mystery, the necessity of mourning from time to time on the journey, that we must trust to God's grace.

I am not detached from these losses. I have a friend who has the gift of tears, who is able to cry with others, to grieve with those who mourn. And she says most wisely, "Let it go. If not this, then God has something better."

We are not to judge someone else, no matter how great our hurt. We may never know how great the temptation was for someone to do exactly what she did. Letting go, forgiveness, accomplished so gradually through the painful yet healing length of days and years, and the daring to turn to others whom we still trust in, can help mend the cracks in us.

I recall that often quoted poem:

> He drew a circle that shut me out—
>   Heretic, rebel, a thing to flout.
> But love and I had the wit to win...
>   We drew a circle that took him in.

The truth in it, however, is much more subtle and less clear than I had thought. Love in us, Christ in us, does not always allow us to bring about the reconciliation on earth that we desire; the other person's free will can never be disregarded.

Rather, the circle that we somehow draw is often imperceptible to the world, and inclusive in a mysterious way that discounts the free will of neither person, but is love suspended. Such love, that does not deny the truth or limit the options of the future, may be present and active, but hidden in Christ.

Love himself, Christ the Friend, is at that center for anyone who chooses his way, the way of the cross. He is the cross, the crux of any decision to include another, to admit grace to the relationship, for the sake of love and what it may yet do to change *us*. To turn away from his offer of friendship that binds friend to friend is like choosing the wrong road at the intersection, traveling the wrong direction, a sidetrack, a backtrack.

In *The Interior Castle* St. Teresa writes, "Our Lord asks but two things of us: love for him and for our neighbour: these are what we must strive to obtain. If we practice both those virtues perfectly we shall be united to Him."

When we accept friendships openly, we also open ourselves to loss. "It is permissible to take life's blessings with both hands," says Meister Eckhart, "provided thou dost know thyself prepared in the opposite event to take them just as gladly. This applies to food and friends and kindred, to anything God gives and takes away....As long as God is satisfied do thou rest content."

For us—in the imperfection of ourselves, our circumstances, our times—the bridging of two wills in harmony and lasting commitment is a miracle when it does occur. Yet in our life with God we are to expect such miracles, to discern rightly when friendship *has* faltered, and to live in the truth.

Kierkegaard has written in his *Journals*, "It requires moral courage to grieve; it requires religious courage to rejoice." And so we are sometimes called upon to count our losses, and to go on with others who abide in friendship with us, in the life we are given, by grace.

LOOKING AT FRIENDSHIP

1. What role do you generally play in the denouement of a friendship? Are you quick to take its pulse and declare it dead, or are you someone who may hang on too long in false hope?

   Each friendship has its own story, shape, duration, and special gifts. Even stories that end in loss have yielded their memories, their richness, to our lives.

2. To acknowledge that even friendship with another Christian may be impermanent is to face a difficult truth. How does this knowledge subtly affect our willingness to risk again, our pleasure in what has been, our admission that we are part of imperfect friendships that are still sustained by grace?

CHAPTER TEN

Mentors as Friends

M aria Harris, in *Dance of the Spirit*, writes of the role of "mentoring" in the lives of the young. The term, she says, derives from the greek myths, and describes the goddess Pallas Athena in her teaching and guidance of the young man Telemachus. Harris speaks of the friendship, usually between generations, that is wrought between mentor and pupil as a kind of "generativity," in the words of Erik Erikson. She prefers the parallel term "traditioning":

"It is the action of handing on and handing over that is the tradition," she writes, not the words, rules, or doctrines themselves that a mentor may pass on to another person. *"Traditioning* is the music of an ancient religious song. We can find the song as far back as Plato; we can find it in the mysticism of Hildegard and Mechtilde....'The Good overflows itself, the Good overflows itself'; *Bonum sui diffusivum est,* 'the Good is that which, by its very nature, has to be diffused and shared.'"

Not all mentors are teachers by vocation, though teachers are usually among the most significant mentor-friends who come to mind. The author Madeleine L'Engle, who has been to me a teacher, mentor, and friend, is one with this tradition of generosity of spirit that allows "the good we have learned to dance in our own lives" to carry over to others.

As a writer and speaker, she refers often to that step of "letting go" that is part of the process of art as well as of love. There is the point at which we realize we cannot be dictators of our own lives, controlling all their aspects. And in the relaxation of that need, the good does overflow, friendship blossoms, life becomes possible for us and for those around us. This letting go in her own life, and its effect on me, is an instance of traditioning, of mentoring, that is a gift of true friendship.

I first encountered the works of Madeleine L'Engle when I was just out of college, working as a curriculum editor. I had not discovered her children's books such as *A Wrinkle in Time*, or *A Wind in the Door*, or any of the Austin family books. But that year, when a colleague took *Wrinkle* out of the library for me, handed it to me with a due date and said, "READ IT!" my fascination with her imaginative works began. Here was a Christian writer who, in her award-winning book, extolled the glories of creation, describing a universe in which glorious creatures sing unending praise to God: "Sing unto the Lord a new song...give glory unto the Lord!" She spoke boldly of a world in which "all things work together for good," and introduced a whole generation to stories in which the ever-present realities of good and evil, and the battle between them, go on incessantly.

She shows us one scenario of the battle with what her character Mrs. Which informs us is: "Eevill. Itt iss thee Ppowers of Ddarrkkness!" And she entices us to follow along in a story that begins in an ordinary world of home and play that we experience every day, and carries us with its heroes and heroine far beyond our dreams and hopes.

There is a section in *Wrinkle* on what one might call mentors—those leaders who inspire us and provide exemplars for us in the art of how to live: how to work, and how to love. She calls them our "chief fighters in the battle....[For] 'the light shineth in darkness; and the darkness comprehended it not.'" And to those lights, those mentors in the spirit of truth, many of us add Madeleine herself, for offering us such a fresh and compelling look at the drama of redemption and our roles as fighters together against the darkness. Such a story, in her hands, in the light of a "sanctified imagination," wraps us up, traditions us, and lets the good overflow.

I don't believe, after I read this book, that I sat down and thought, "Here is a mentor for me in my own aspirations to write and open doors for other people because of my Christian belief." But in Madeleine I had encountered someone so creative and bold that her works cannot be ignored or the ideas in them discounted, even by the skeptical. And she speaks in the widest circles of storytelling, not just to an elite audience that shares Christian language, but to all sons of Adam and daughters of Eve.

I first met Madeleine L'Engle on a day she experienced great uncertainty, pain, and testing. I was working as a book editor for a publishing company in the Chicago area, and Madeleine was to have lunch with our executive editor and me while she was in town speaking at the local college. We wanted to talk to her about her poetry and her religious writings after *The Irrational Season*—particularly her reflections on creation, on *beginnings*, which have since been published as a series on Genesis.

My boss and I joined her in our reception area, and we got ready to leave for a restaurant. She told us immediately that she had just received word from New York that her young granddaughter and namesake had been hit by a truck the day before and was hospitalized. At that moment, the child's condition was uncertain, and no one knew whether she had sustained brain damage from the accident. Adding further anxiety to the situation, a blackout in New York had left the phone lines dead, and no word was immediately available on Léna's condition.

Yet Madeleine L'Engle, full of prayer and watchfulness, kept our lunch engagement, kept going, giving, thinking, feeling—ever mindful of the presence of the unknown outcome hanging over herself, her family, and this loved one. To us, as new friends and potential colleagues, it revealed the dignity and authenticity of her faith in a most trying situation.

We can never choose the conditions under which we will be required to act on our beliefs, and when we are vocal about our faith it seems we are often put to the test in the most public of ways. For Madeleine, this was an opportunity to ask for prayer from the Christian community in which she was currently speaking and serving. And in the process, the good of our connections with each other in Christ could be tested, expanded.

It is this kind of faith—in the dark, in the uncertainty of outcome—that opens us up rather than closes us off to others. And it is that trust in God's goodness, in God's purposes for all creation, that always shines strongest in the dark—or in the words of Charles Williams (whose name came up among us at that very table), "Faith in a bag is faith at its best."

Madeleine's granddaughter, after months of treatment and recovery, and great personal courage, did recover fully. But we had seen Madeleine herself caught in time, between knowing and not knowing, yet still giving. It was her own example that provided the "traditioning," a revelation of how it is to live as a Christian, that spoke louder than words. The good that overflowed was her sense of peace within, the conviction of God's goodness that also informs her work, and that clearly held her in that hour.

This lunch meeting was for me the fulfillment of a hope to meet someday the author of *A Wrinkle in Time* as a real working writer, talking shop, sharing ideas, seeing some of the seeds of works in an author's mind that would be watered and nurtured to produce results. I remember feeling a certain awe simply from being in her presence, though it was soon dispelled by the directness and honesty of her manner. It was clear that Madeleine, already an award-winning, acclaimed author, could have rested on past successes. But here she was, still taking risks by branching into new forms of expression, reaching new readers through ever more honest explorations of her faith and her life, with more explicit witness to her Christian belief.

Though our company did not end up working with L'Engle on that particular project, I was to begin a correspondence and an acquaintance that day that would become a friendship. Here was the opportunity to learn from the very mentor I most needed to sustain the courage and vision to go on in my own work, especially my fledgling and frustrating writing efforts.

We were to meet again several years later when Madeleine was teaching summer school at Mundelein College, where I was earning a masters in Religious Studies. This time another accident had occurred and Madeleine arrived in a wheelchair, having tripped over a cardboard cat carrier just before she was to leave for this teaching stint. Not one to let a cast, crutches, or the wheelchair get in her way, she kept her commitment to those of us who had eagerly signed up for her writing seminar, "Writing as Spiritual Nurture."

Besides the personal inconveniences and pain of recovery, a wheelchair meant for her a loss of independence and mobility. It took her longer to get to class with friends pushing her along, special care on elevators, through hallways, and down Chicago streets. If that were not enough, I remember that it rained quite a bit during those two weeks. My friend Anita, who was also taking the course and earning a degree along with me, remembers the occasion as a sort of magical scenario, our umbrella'd Mary Poppins-like teacher and mentor being wheelchair-bound, but her ideas and liveliness dancing above us and carrying the day.

I remember walking along with her entourage, helping with books and papers, carrying on conversations—and seeing in Madeleine not an inkling of self-pity or anger, any apologetic spirit or martyrdom. She was simply Madeleine (in one slice of normal life, its ills and pains along with its joys) being Madeleine at what she does best: sharing the Good News.

I kept in touch with Madeleine in letters, telling her about changes in my life and the few articles I was able to publish here and there. I went to hear her speak whenever she was in our area (always hoping and sometimes finding a few minutes alone with her); and she, years later, came to our parish in Chicago, at my husband, the rector's, request, to speak in the service and then spend an afternoon at our home.

Several years ago the time and place finally became right for me to attempt my first book. My editorial career was on hold, though I still worked freelance. I was keeping a journal, and I finally found the focus to attempt a full-length work. It was Advent, a church season for which Madeleine and I share a love, and I was expecting my first child.

I sent Madeleine early drafts of some of the chapters and later on I asked her if she would write an introduction to it. My final draft reached her at another crisis time in her life. As she says in the introduction: "Isabel Anders wrote these Advent meditations while waiting for her first baby to be born. I read them in my husband's hospital room, watching him die. Now another Advent approaches, another time when birth and death draw close together and it is not always possible to tell which is which."

Once again, through great personal pain, she continued to give of herself to me and to readers. In this gift of her words, a legacy of her friendship, I experienced the joy of seeing some of our thoughts entwined, our personal experiences casting light on each other's. Of the chapter in the book in which I contrasted "summery spirituality" with "wintery spirituality," Madeleine writes, "Like her, I tend to identify with the wintry view....Strangely I have found in my own life that it is only through a wintry spirituality that I am able to affirm summer and sunshine." Madeleine's words reflect her life, her perseverance as woman and writer in her task of telling her own ongoing story.

It has been said that if we truly love something, it is inevitable that we become somehow a part of it. I would like to think that the love of beauty, of truth, of the good, of the incarnational vehicle of language is itself a milieu that often draws us to those we most need to meet and know and learn from. Love is the connection between friends, between teacher and learner, mentor and pupil.

When I think of Madeleine and all that she offers her readers, her audiences, her many friends and fellow writers, I think of her honesty and her willingness to give of herself generously. A window into the mind and art of such a person is an opening to the hope and the possibility of also being able to pass on hard-won experience. To believe in and follow the tradition of mentoring is to affirm the example of what one voice can bring into the world for good.

I respect Madeleine for the credit she gives to her Creator for her work and any good that comes out of it. In her introduction to a new edition of Dorothy L. Sayers's book on creativity, *The Mind of the Maker*, L'Engle writes:

"When I am asked how long it takes me to write a book, the answer is trinitarian: (1) when I start actually putting the words on paper; (2) when the idea of the book first came to me; (3) when I was born, before I was actually aware of any particular book. The ideas and metaphors for a book start long before we are actually aware of them."

In this she echoes Nicholas Berdyaev:

"God created man in his own image and likeness, i.e., made him a creator too, calling him to free spontaneous activity and not to formal obedience to His power. Free creativeness is the creature's answer to the great call of its Creator. Man's creative work is the fulfilment of the Creator's secret will."

This, for L'Engle, is the source of the good that overflows; it is God. And cooperating with this process is not only a "letting go," but also a discipline and an act of free will. It is daring to become a co-creator, sharing in all the risks and pain—and potential joy—of birth. Nothing could be more natural; and it is this entering into the cycle, the tradition, that connects friend with friend.

To find the exceptional good fortune of a mentor who is also a friend is to know someone who answers letters, returns calls, asks about your life as well as tells of his or her own, finds your work of value, but is able to give constructive criticism, too. Such a person knows how to take compliments and give them; sees people as individuals, remembers names, asks about needs, and is faithful in love and prayer.

One pitfall is to continue in awe of a mentor who seems so far above what you can attain. The challenge is to be yourself with dignity and assert your own place without fuss or undue pushiness. Sometimes this means to disagree, to challenge and press a point in dialogue, as equals. Madeleine is one, I have found, who welcomes such counterpoint and suggestions, and thus friendship only grows.

To know such a person as mentor and friend is an instance of grace, of the wide range of possibilities of friendship when one is open to such a gift. In an interview on friendship I once did with Madeleine for the book *Practical Christianity*, I asked her, "Should friendship be between people who are equals?" She answered, "Certainly there should be a high degree of mutuality in friendship. We are never exact equals with our friends. But there is a certain interdependence you create, in which you each give different gifts. If you are overly dependent in a relationship, you tend to idolize the other person, and then you are asking of that person something that should be asked only of God."

She wisely warns against the idolatry of such friendships and the danger to both parties. From the standpoint of one who sees in her a flesh-and-blood mentor, I see how easy it would be to underestimate one's own gifts and miss the opportunity for whatever reciprocity can exist. It is a challenge in such a friendship to be oneself without shrinking away self-consciously, or drawing too much attention to inequalities. This in itself partakes of the courtesy of friendship.

A mentor may be a friend from a distance, such as a "psychological mentor" whose thought influences us from books and teachings, but whom we never meet. This is of necessity a limited, one-sided experience. Friends of pages we read are often such mentors (see Chapter Twelve), but there is a much more exciting, dynamic dimension when we can know such a mentor personally.

We should never hesitate to praise anyone who has touched us for good. But we can overpraise mentors, or overflatter for our own gain, if we are not careful. This does them as great a disservice as it does to us and our growth and our place in the story. We can also be too timid and miss the opportunity for friendship altogether. It takes grace to maintain friendship with people at all levels of achievement and to keep proper perspective on our own gifts and those of others.

I speak of the area of writing and literature because it is what I know. But this must be true in many fields, wherever some excel and are recognized above their peers.

Now as the years pass, I sometimes find the tables turned (how could I have become old enough to be a mentor?) as people come to me for advice on their writing, not now as an editor but as an author. Recently I had the opportunity to read some poetry and articles written by a young woman in our community; based on the promise I saw in her, I helped her get a job as feature editor at our local paper. I feel proud and somehow a participant when I see her column with her picture appear weekly! It's surprising to me how much it feels like being a mother—an example of "generativity" at work, of freely offering something of what one is and knows, and seeing it live in a totally new form, totally "other" and separate from me. I'm not responsible for what Kit writes in her column, but as a mentor and friend, I share in the satisfaction.

LOOKING AT FRIENDSHIP

1. What friendships among "unequals" have been part of your experience of the journey to this point? How have your mentors changed along the way? How have you?

   C. S. Lewis said that "hierarchy" is more like a dance than a drill. Finding our place as friends among our peers and mentors may also be a more fluid state of being than we thought.

2. What is your responsibility as mentor to those who may look up to you in your family, work, vocation, community?

The Spiritual Director and Friendship

I n the "Peanuts" cartoon series, the character Lucy frequently sets herself up in a little sidewalk booth, offering advice for five cents to her playmates. Charlie Brown is usually her best, and neediest, customer. In one episode in which she gives her candid opinion on his plight, Lucy asks, "Discouraged again, eh, Charlie Brown? You know what your trouble is?"

He continues to stare bleakly into the distance. But she persists:

"The whole trouble with you is that you're you!"

Even though it is only a cartoon, it conveys the message that our circumstances, other people, and even our culture sometimes force us to accept. A spiritual friend, on the other hand, will help us to see what *is* acceptable in us, our assets as well as our shortcomings, and will side with us on the journey to greater wholeness, from whatever point at which we begin to believe.

One such spiritual friend is called in Christian tradition a "spiritual director." A spiritual director is someone experienced in the life of prayer, usually able to be a confessor, and is of like mind with the person seeking direction. Through the discipline of regular meetings, difficulties and the different stages of progress are revealed to the director honestly, in a spirit of humility and openness.

A friend with whom you share your desire for growth, as well as your need for guidance and companionship, is perhaps the most intentional of friends outside the taking of vows of marriage or religious vocation. Spiritual guidance starts with the premise that you are, before God, exactly who God designed you to be. And all that God has created is good.

Spiritual direction in the Christian tradition is an opportunity for the development of one of the most intensely healing of friendships, so such a friend should be chosen carefully after much prayer. While friendships with family, neighbors, and close associates are often "givens," to make of what you will, rather than freely chosen, the selection of a mentor with whom to share one's journey opens up another dimension altogether.

To travel alongside a spiritual guide (for the relationship should be one of recognized equality in personal worth and responsibility, if not in experience) is to discover another facet of the school of love. To be instructed in prayer while on the path of everyday living is to allow oneself the deep scrutiny and touch of the Spirit in all areas of life. But through these steps in quest of the more committed life, it means not to walk alone. Aelred of Rievaulx wrote of those souls under his direction: "You know, Lord, my intention is not so much to be their superior as to lovingly help them and humbly serve them, to be, at their side, one of them...." And he saw that such friendship is "like a step to raise us to the love and knowledge of God...."

It is as though the underlying basis of all Christian friendship is made clearer, God's purposes for our connections with others more transparent, in this partnership of mentor and pupil in the way of prayer. The ongoing choice to be guided by what St. Francis calls a "faithful friend," demands that a director be "full of charity, of knowledge, and of prudence; if one of these three qualities is wanting...there is danger."

I am not sure when I first heard of the possibility of finding such a relationship, of taking the step of opening up the private domain of my spiritual life to another more schooled in the tradition and practice of the life of prayer. It has become a way of accountability and specific guidance for me in my personal as well as my professional life as a writer. Choosing to develop, under direction, greater discipline in prayer, and learning to discern God's will in my life, has meant to allow myself to experience both the pain and the joys of walking with another. To place myself under the guidance of a wiser and more experienced woman (in my case), means to be in close touch with one who can help me see what I lack and how God is calling me to *more* rather than less, a fullness rather than deprivation or diminishment.

Sharing the stages of inner growth with a succession of spiritual friends—for their faces have changed as I have moved around the country—has a certain pattern. At the center and crux of the experience, I have found the rightness of *attending to where I am* on the journey. I have been able to take time to reflect and often to act, at crucial points along the road, with another person there beside me. At the times of my most critical needs to make decisions and adjust to new obstacles, opportunities, heartaches—my spiritual guide has ever been a point of dependability and support, a faithful companion on the journey of friendship with Christ. I have found that what begins as placing oneself *under* a wise guide can lead to an increasing experience of friendship that is *alongside* another, though one's gifts may never be equal.

I knew quite quickly, after my first meetings with Sister Penelope, that spiritual direction was right for me to begin at that time, as a lifelong choice. When I think of initially arriving at the retreat center to meet with her (the guide is often, but not always, a member of a religious community), all I remember is the beauty of the surroundings shining through to reach me in the painful experience of "losing my way" spiritually. After the loss of another person I had looked up to in a very close relationship, I felt truly in the wilderness, without direction.

The threshold to approaching things of the Spirit is the physical world in which we dwell and which was declared by God to be good. We meet with another in a definite time and place, usually apart from our daily work and living. In this instance, after entering the spacious grounds and driving across a small bridge, I parked the car and walked across an autumn lawn strewn with wet leaves, down a path, through a mild twilight, and these words from C. S. Lewis's *That Hideous Strength* came unbidden to me:

"Jane went out of the big house...into the liquid night and supernatural warmth of the garden and across the wet lawn (birds were everywhere) and past the seesaw and the greenhouse and the piggeries, going down all the time...descending the ladder of humility."

I realize now that my experience was similar to that of many people in the recovery movement, of acknowledging a Higher Power. Though I had long believed in my relationship to God and sought to live as a Christian, I had found myself failing, unable to cope in the chaotic circumstances of my life. I was clearly being sent to my knees, to a place of expectancy and hope, from which the only direction to look was up. For me, seeking a spiritual director was both a symbol and an action of turning to God again.

Recognizing the beauty and dignity of our own being, choosing to move toward the center of God's friendship, the will of Christ for us, is also always both a fresh choice to live in reality, and an exercise in humility. It took me a long time even to attempt to express the relationship between this sense of the beauty in all that God has made and the choices that the soul makes in spiritual direction. I couldn't connect my experience of the walk that evening with the spiritual longings that accompanied it.

In seeking such guidance, it is as though you are within a shell that has just been cracked open to the light. Not only is your pain exposed, but also your ability to perceive through the senses the many gifts of life and beauty—the canopy of the sky, the trees that shade, the sources of water and the fruits of the earth—that surround you and that may have been taken for granted in normal, sequential daily life.

I thought at first that the vast and well-kept grounds of the convent were like icing on the cake, an almost frivolous present to compel me on the way, or to lift me into a state of awareness and receptivity. But I see now that what I discovered on the way to seek spiritual direction was simply the experience of my common humanity—as one who seeks God in the cool of the evening, as did the first man and woman in the Garden of Eden. For where else can we seek God but in the local plot of earth from where we first admit our need, our poverty? What is important is that we are able to look around us and to look up.

I see now that the act of simply putting one foot after the other was the only obedience required of me at the time—seeking guidance through an ancient and accepted tradition of the church. For another it might take an entirely different shape. I am grateful that, through the advice of my priest, there was something I could do in the face of loss, the hope of new understanding in my continued quest for wholeness.

Apprenticeship to a spiritual director is not lessons in ethics or even in the growth of the soul. It is the immersion of the whole person in a school of testing that will have implications for every aspect of one's life. The body and its needs, one's physical environment and its demands, are all part of the picture and are never considered trivial by the spiritual guide—who also should be rooted in the reality of human community and experience.

James Nelson writes in *The Intimate Connection*:

"When ethics loses its attention to flesh-and-blood concreteness, then bloodless abstractions, principles, and concepts begin to take on a life of their own. They become more real than people, animals, plants, and earth. What is lost, however, is not only concreteness but also the sense of connection—the deep, bodily sense of our profound connectedness to everything else.

"The recovery of the body," he continues, "brings with it the realization that the fundamental reality of our lives is not our separation but our relatedness."

This is part of the rich truth that the experience of spiritual direction has taught me, through the wise guides who have seen and affirmed this connectedness with me, in the moment, and of us all in God's care. The spiritual guide always begins with who you really are, encourages you to express truths about yourself, and assists in the peeling off, layer by layer, of your false self. It is only as yourself, in acceptance of your being in that moment, this moment—that you can offer your presence and share with another what you have to give.

Seeking another person as guide entails some planning, in that it usually involves appointments, often in a small room of quiet and peace; sometimes in a chapel where the practice of prayer accompanies any discussion of the subject. When meetings with a spiritual guide take the form of a retreat, there is usually a movement back and forth from the presence of the other, to solitude and prayer, study and rest, to allow God to use the carefully chosen words and instructions you have been given to feed on.

In Sister Penelope I found a rather stern love, a sureness of purpose as she led me into a discipline of prayer. Yet I also discovered a kindness of heart and her solicitude for every detail of my schedule: reading the Bible, praying, resting, eating, and sleeping. Clearly no detail was outside her scrutiny or care, and I felt somewhat kindly corralled into a sheltered and blessedly ordered way of life for the few days of retreat. It was both comforting (in that I was required to make few decisions myself) and a bit daunting, as I felt my own personal disorder more sharply in her strong presence. It was not unusual to see her frown as I revealed particularly difficult thoughts to her, or to hear her praying softly—perhaps in tongues—when we knelt together at the altar rail.

It is important to remember that such guidance always takes place in real time and space, often not far from a window on the beauties of creation, and with allowance for our human limits and frailty. Sometimes it involves staying at a retreat house overnight, in a room where there are few distractions, and prayer and solitude can be realized. This description of such a room in Susan Howatch's novel *Glittering Images*, strikes a chord in me, reminding me of similar experiences:

"I sat down very suddenly on the bed. The room was small and neat, the bed placed in the corner, the table and chair by the window, the wardrobe against the inner wall, the basin in another corner by the unlit gas fire. There were no curtains, only a black blind, and no pictures. On the bedside table stood a lamp and a Bible." Such spareness is a gift—the absence of details and demands that our day-to-day lives usually contain. Like rich food, a generous portion of spiritual fare may prove too much to digest in one session. We are encouraged by our guide to space out our intake and to include rest and recovery in our daily work.

Either pain or joy, or both intermingled, can be our impetus to seek a spiritual guide. Usually our motive arises from a unique combination of need and plenitude, confusion and challenge. Often we come with a desire, as I had, for a stronger dose of the delights already tasted in solitude and in community. Sometimes our initial prayer, as we start out on such a quest, is almost as held in balance as this prayer/poem by William Cowper:

> O make this heart rejoice, or ache;
>   Decide this doubt for me;
> And if it be not broken, break,
>   And heal it if it be.

Spiritual inquiry is that seeking for something more—help in unlocking secrets that another may have already discovered, but that will have a new flavor when encountered together. To know the companionship spoken of in Psalm 133, the pleasures of living together in unity, is to find spiritual friendship "like precious oil poured on the head...as if the dew of Hermon were falling on Mount Zion" (vv. 1-3). The wholeness that can be known in moments of such a friendship is indeed palpable, an oil of gladness, but it is also an anointing of responsibility. When we are helped to see both our gifts and our failings, the blessings and woundedness of our own particular life, we can no longer claim ignorance. We have been touched by another and by God's spirit in a way that requires us to give back, in yet unspecified ways—never to be forced or hurried—at a later point on our journey.

In choosing to open up our hearts and wills to a spiritual mentor, we have given over an important trust. We allow someone else to uncover some of our wounds—inevitable in any life fully lived—to make them bare in the warmth and honesty of acceptance and love, in order to find healing together. For the guide who walks with us is human and vulnerable as well, and one who is also being formed and reformed by God's Spirit. The best spiritual guide is one who has already been wounded and found strength through the assistance and love of another. It is one who has discovered that balm, that oil of healing which can only expand when it is shared, ever overflowing like the supernatural bounty of the widow's jar, blessed by the prophet.

Because spiritual direction requires a balance of solitude and unity, a person with that gift is often found within a community suited to nurturing such a vocation. These retreat houses, set aside for worship and prayer, and for just such spiritual friendship, may seem at first to be Camelots in the desert of secular life. But one soon learns that life in community has all the strains and demands of life outside, wherever people's wills are not in perfect harmony—that is, anywhere under the sun. Weeds grow even in convent gardens; spiritual direction is not only a question of prayer and contemplation, but also of social life. "The adjustment of domestic duties requires as much discernment as turning a point in mental prayer," in the words of F. W. Faber. Although going back to "ordinary" life is sometimes a jolt, we face it with the strength gained from an intense period of reflection that has allowed for such a return.

Spiritual guides are friends in times of great need and also in times of rest and refreshment, times of dryness and defeat, and of victories along the way. They have seen in their own lives how the seasons of the soul progress and turn, year to year, and they are undaunted by these changes, seeing them as a natural part of the path—for "all the way to heaven is heaven," in the words of one saint.

In the course of our reliance on such a friend, there also arises at some point a need for detachment, even from dependence on such a friend. Though he or she may be there for you in your deepest need and most honest seeking after God, there is always a point at which the guide can do no more until you take the steps that are required of you next before God.

Twice in the past five years, my experience of spiritual direction has been interrupted—once by moving away and the second time by my director's need for physical recovery and a lightened burden of direction. Such changes require, for both people in the relationship, an adjustment to absence. Distance serves to emphasize our separateness and our individual responsibility before God—as well as our care, from where we are, for the ongoing well-being of the other. New circumstances bring new duties. Sometimes we must "fly" on our own for a scary span of days. Or we may be led to a new relationship with a guide who can be part of our life in a changed situation.

I have been trying now, for many months, to write a letter to my former spiritual director. But I have found it impossible to transfer to paper what needs to be said—thus realizing again, each time I try, what the loss of her personal presence and the taste of that gift of her guidance meant and still means to me. It has been a further humbling experience, and a trust that this, too, is one of the lessons of love.

Any spiritual guide is limited, as we are. Yet in their vocations, by God's grace, they are offering something beyond themselves, the deep wells of the Spirit as a refreshment and a source of fellowship. Our choice of how to respond, what to do next at any point, is a freedom that they respect and value. This also is the sign of a true spiritual friend.

In choosing a spiritual director, you may find yourself drawn to one because of a similar temperament; perhaps many who seek such a relationship have an affinity with those who exercise that vocation. Harris writes: "It is not unusual for me to learn, after teaching a spirituality course, that women in the course have gone on to work regularly with someone as spiritual director or mentor." And after such an experience, some go on to become directors themselves.

The acceptance of another's understanding of your spiritual state, acknowledging the true nature of your choices at that point, is not subservience, though it may require obedience to a power beyond both people. It is, again, more of a dance than a drill, a seeking for priorities and concrete actions (or patience in inaction) that never denies your equality before God. Rather, someone under direction is willing to set aside, for the benefit of her spirit, her own illusion of being in control of her life—to admit her blindness and insensitivity to her own faults for the sake of what can be gained through instruction.

The mutual *respect, courtesy,* and *gravity* that must accompany one called to the vocation of spiritual guide can help to prevent a manipulative relationship, and instead lead to growth for both director and disciple. I am thankful for those three virtues as they have been reflected in the faces of my several directors, who mirror for me the love of God in Christ.

Respect takes the form of a certain gentleness of inquiry. I think of my second spiritual director, a laywoman who helped me to probe my *own* feelings, rather than stating the obvious and sometimes cruel truth, in the course of direction. *Courtesy* is closely related: she showed gracious consideration for my physical needs as I struggled with spiritual concerns; and yet the *gravity* that she exhibited, in the face of the life-or-death issues with which I struggled, gave the correct tone to a serious and profound dilemma.

In her, as in those other women who have ministered to me in times of extremity and through years of searching, I see beauty. The faces themselves—modest, lovely, intelligent, loving, stern, sympathetic—are real enough, touched by God's grace, as is my own, in its changes through the years.

LOOKING AT FRIENDSHIP

1. What other qualities besides those mentioned—charity, knowledge, prudence, respect, courtesy, and gravity—would you look for as most essential in a spiritual guide and mentor? How do you both encourage and value those virtues in yourself?

   Honesty, charity, patience, clarity, steadfastness, hope...these are the marks of a spiritual friend who can serve to help keep us on the way of love and obedience.

2. How is prayer both an individual and a corporate experience? What are the implications for your friendships of this truth?

CHAPTER TWELVE

Friends Within Pages

My father's stories and his love of passing them on were to open up to me a world of delight and often of guidance far beyond my imagination. They were almost a passport to another country, one from which I could journey back and forth at will, through the magical act of lifting a book and turning its pages.

In his poem "Keepsake" Walter Wangerin writes of such pages:

> Oh, my children! What can I bequeath
> You more than stories? Lips don't last: they dry
> Soon, tremble soon, and die; but they that breathed
> Warm words against your flesh and kissed your eyes—
> That will remain in memory a story.
> All of the goods I leave you you will use
> Up...
> But stories deep as fairy tales, as searching
> As poetry...
> —these stand mining (whether
> I'm dead, ye delvers, or alive) forever—

A friend once told me it was a good thing I had read the "right" books when I was growing up, because I am so much a product of what I have read—"You could have been a bad person if you'd read the wrong things!" Recently I came upon a variation on this idea of "we are what we read" in Jonathan Raban's *For Love and Money: A Writing Life*: "Every work of literature turns the successful collaborative reader of it into its co-author. In an important sense, we write what we read."

I'm not sure which way it really works—whether we are drawn to characters and ideas in books that already fit our view of life (already being formed through our experiences in our families) and enhance it; and thus these become the "right books" for us. Or are the faces and truths we encounter within pages powerful enough to mold some of us for better or worse, to break and remold us by their power as we discover them and continue to delve into their depths?

I do know that faces of friendship within books have been immensely formative of what I call my life, my journey with others, as guideposts, but especially as instances of joy and community along the way: "I'm not the only one who has had an experience like that!" Yet how wonderfully *other* and profoundly different is this particular expression of a thought that connects to my own.... How these insights inspire in me a better response to the circumstances of my own life right now.

Jacques Barzun in *Begin Here* writes of why we should read the classics of literature, though they are often a struggle: "Because a classic is thick and full, and because it arose out of a past situation, it is hard to read. The mental attitude and attention that are good enough for reading the newspaper and most books will not work....But why, after all, learn to read differently by tackling the classics? The answer is simple: in order to live in a wider world....Wider than the one that comes through the routine of our material lives and through the paper and the factual magazines...wider also than friends' and neighbors' plans and gossip; wider especially than one's business or profession. For nothing is more narrowing than one's own shop....Through this experience we escape from the prison cell....It is like gaining a second life."

Novelist Isabel Allende has her heroine in *Eva Luna* write of the gift of stories that her mother Consuelo gave to her: "She placed at my feet the treasures of the Orient, the moon, and beyond. She reduced me to the size of an ant so I could experience the universe from that smallness; she gave me wings to see it from the heavens; she gave me the tail of a fish so I would know the depths of the sea. When she was telling a story, her characters peopled my world....She sowed in my mind the idea that reality is not only what we see on the surface; it has a magical dimension as well and, if we so desire, it is legitimate to enhance it and color it to make our journey through life less trying."

These are not always conscious thoughts we have in reading words and stories that touch us deeply; but they often underlie the experience, as though we are standing with the storyteller, looking at something together and saying, "You, too? I thought I was the only one."

C. S. Lewis wrote in *Surprised by Joy* of an awakening into joy that came in the instant of his discovery of these three lines in Longfellow's translation of Tegner's *Drapa*:

> I heard a voice that cried,
> Balder the beautiful
> Is dead, is dead—

For him it was a sudden embracing of the concept of "northernness" in Norse myth—a coldness, openness, and otherness beyond his personal experience yet touching it—a window into another world, one that makes this one brighter and more bearable. Stories for him, as a child encouraged to read, were a gift he grew to be able to pass on to others, a fact adding to the pleasure and brightness of many of our lives as we have read his childhood classics, the Narnia stories.

Language itself is a vehicle for connecting us, one to the other; the incarnation of thought, something Walker Percy calls the "Delta factor." He writes in *The Message in the Bottle*:

"In the beginning was Alpha and the end is Omega, but somewhere between occurred Delta, which was nothing less than the arrival of man himself and his breakthrough into the daylight of language and consciousness and knowing, of happiness and sadness, of being with and being alone, of being right and being wrong, of being himself and being not himself, and of being at home and being a stranger."

These are the paradoxes of story, of communicating our lives to each other. They also describe succinctly the human condition, which all our tales in some way reflect, as best as we are able.

Why do certain images and thoughts from others' minds resonate in us and generate further growth, open our worlds, and make us aware of ourselves among others in a new way?

I remember in my early years of reading, being stopped and held by stories of home, of contentment with smallness, snug and complete as the hole of a fox or the tidy, swept cottage of Mrs. Beaver in Lewis's own *The Lion, the Witch and the Wardrobe*. It was a discovery, not of openness or vastness, but of the joy of containment, of "beauty within bounds," a phrase I have since been unable to locate exactly. (I have since read somewhere that it is not unusual for men to dream of openness and vastness, while women conceive of shape and enclosure in their images of self.)

The peace within, the joy of containedness is echoed in the words of Psalm 101: "I will walk with sincerity of heart within my house" (v. 2). And the image of the house, of refuge and stability, is often, in the psalms, enlarged on in the more exalted image of Zion, the city of God:

> Jerusalem is built as a city
>   that is at unity with itself.
> ...Peace be within your walls
>   and quietness within your towers.
>   (Ps. 122:3, 7)

Perhaps in my mind the image of security in one's abode has something to do with the quiet of an only-child household, or the fact that my father was in the building trades. Collected together, these are all at once images of solitude and of community, of activity and of repose—all that goes on in the well-oiled household.

Finding our place in the world, in the midst of others, particularly our own family, has everything to do with preparation for that journey to God's household, to which at present we are both pilgrims and strangers. For me, it brings to mind God's work to enable each person to fulfill his own destiny within the Kingdom.

No one has written so beautifully of this concept as the British missionary to India, Amy Carmichael, one of the friends within pages who helped shape my own early response to the beauty and wisdom of the language of Scripture, our best guide to the journey home. In *His Thoughts Said...His Father Said...* she writes of the son asking why such special tools are used in forming the stone for God's house in Jerusalem, why the preparation time is so extended, and the chiseling process often so severe:

> His father said, The house, when it was in building, was built of stone made ready before it was brought thither; so that there was neither hammer nor axe nor any tool of iron heard in the house, while it was in building.

> If thou knewest the disappointment it is to the builders when the stone cannot be used for the house, because it was not made ready...if thou knewest My purpose for thee, thou wouldest welcome any tool if only it prepared thee quietly and perfectly to fit into thy place in the house.

The shaping of the individual, the personal growth of each stone within the edifice is truly connected to the whole. The one finds a place among the many. Salvation is both individual and corporate, and the City is in preparation even now.

The best literature that I have been drawn to, especially within the Christian tradition, underlines this particularity within universality, the paradox of being and walking alone, yet always with and for others, in the shadow of the saints, the company of the whole Body of Christ.

That such unity of minds, such friendship, can exist across generations, and we can influence for good someone whom we have never known personally, is one of the miracles of reading, especially within the tradition of devotion and spirituality.

Other faces from pages I have known appear before me: all of the sisters in *Little Women* (a book I read at least five times, unwilling to leave that world); the heroines and heroes of Shakespeare, and later, the characters of *Till We Have Faces* and C. S. Lewis's other works of fiction, Charles Williams's characters in his seven novels, the faces in the novels of Iris Murdoch, Robertson Davies, and countless others, ancient and modern.

Each person, each face, reflects some aspect of humanity as we encounter it in ourselves and in others—Jo's (of *Little Women*) independence, Isabel's (in Williams's *Shadows of Ecstasy*) wholeness in submission, Jane's (of Lewis's *That Hideous Strength*) vision. The completion of the City requires each of us, reflecting what we can of Christ, of the myriad varieties of creation. Often a character portrays, instead, the denial of good and of unity. Some of the most horrifying faces of denial do appear in these novels by Christian authors who could see the choice that each soul faces, the terror and opportunity of the crossroads, of taking this way or that. Each person walks either toward the unity of the City of God—which begins in this life— or fosters the degradation of the image of God within.

The basis of unity, as many of these authors saw—is personal integrity, the clarity of one's face in reflecting what it is to be human before God, along with others. When such connection is lacking, denied, the result is a downward spiral, unforgettably painted in the damnation of Weston in *Out of the Silent Planet*, or of Wentworth in *Descent into Hell*. In the masterful hands of such writers as Lewis and Williams, there is always, even in a "mere story," something of the sense of warning and admonition underlying scenes of such faces and their fates. As did the authors' mentor Dante, in his *Divine Comedy*, they tell us through story and myth that we can yet be molded this way or that while we are still in time and have choices ourselves. Today is always the day of salvation.

Yes, I suppose that what we read, if we are attentive, does help make us what we are. For me, the earliest true delight I remember, the thing that I liked best and that liked me back, was ideas. The less obvious the story in its intent, the more complex the web of faces and relationships within the pages, the greater the challenge.

There is more than one way to learn from the experience of others and from literature than the way of didacticism. It is possible to step back, not needing to be told exactly what this means "for my life right now." Our encounters with obscurity and complexity, the mixed messages that other people (and characters within pages) give us, are also part of our preparation, the forming of ourselves. What we read makes up a part of the journey. It can lighten (and make, lighter) our way.

In Scripture, that book so important since my childhood, I find faces of friends for the journey. Especially in the psalms I always seem to recognize the territory, as I read of the psalmists' own encounters with real enemies who dig ditches and send warriors against their peace, as well as the marvelous affirmations of praise and truth directed to God in the midst of the day-to-day battle.

The psalms themselves swing back and forth from the pivot points of personal integrity and God's overall purpose in creation. Their use in worship, too, has always been one of the personal and the corporate, as individual voices joined in unison, an ancient body of diverse faces that sang as one for the duration of the response of praise.

Encountering friends within pages is part of the joy of being in the community of believers, to mingle among the greatest minds, and know friends of the enduring written page. "These stand mining...forever."

How does one come to put so much stock in friends among pages? Books are an invitation to enter another's world, to suspend the laws of time and space temporarily to see what new dimension might open up. To paraphrase Lewis, a young person cannot be too careful about what she reads, what the eye may fall on, open books, "fine nets and stratagems" opening out to beauty, or entrapment. It is a risk, what we choose to read, and to be a collaborative reader puts us practically into the story itself. Silently it says to us, "Come along...."

A willing reader at the threshold of such an invitation stands at the beginning of a kind of friendship with the world, one that can open up into an ever-larger reality, into a love of much that is beyond the self and yet touches one intimately. The connections we can make with lives lived in the past, with lives never lived except on pages, and the ways in which we live through such words—all of this sends the message to me that it is a world enspirited, peopled, designed, a world in which two gifts stand out, reflecting God's image: our ability to create and our ability to choose.

I am drawn to the inexhaustible treasures of literature in which friends of the mind and spirit have been found—not only to their imaginative works, but to fragments of biographical information that help me see them as human beings. It is a privilege to observe them speaking and hearing the voices of their times and learning of the works of other writers that were available to them.

Lewis's love of his mentor George MacDonald's writings was so great that he wrote the wise preacher in as a character in one of his own books (*The Great Divorce*). Though they never met in time, their stories thus become entwined. Such friendships *connect* past with present, reader with writer, idea with idea.

Another important mentor/friend whom I have known only within pages, is the Anglican writer of many works on spirituality, Evelyn Underhill, of whom it was said the two things most important to her were praying and writing. It is almost as though she didn't need to mention *reading*, it was so obvious. As a young girl she wrote in her little black notebook of herself: "Amongst the poets I prefer Shakespeare for general excellence,

Milton for majesty, Tennyson and Keats for beautiful thoughts, musically set...."

In those early days, long before her vocation was clear, she wrote, "As to religion, I don't quite know, except that I believe in a God, and think it is better to love and help the poor people round me than to go on saying that I love an abstract Spirit whom I have never seen. If I can do both, all the better, but it is best to begin with the nearest."

While her gifts in writing turn on the finest of abstract thought and analysis of the spiritual life in a classical sense, she also saw the importance of the particular faces in her life, and her relation to them before God, as the essence of true spirituality.

In these writers, and in life, I enjoy the dance back and forth from the faces around us to the abstractions that connect ideas and make reality more accessible to us for further examined living. These faces of friendship—the authors and the characters they have created—do that for me still.

Poet George Herbert writes in his prose work "The Country Parson" of this "commerce of knowledge"—the sharing of one's treasure of ideas with others—"that there may be a traffic in knowledge between the servants of God, for the planting both of love, and humility." In his poem "The Windows," Herbert compares the believer to a stained glass window. These works of art often tell a story, keep it alive visually, pass it on. Herbert sees their truth as a complement to the words of the preacher, words that do teach more directly, but not always effectively in that "glorious and transcendent place," the temple of God. What is needed to enliven doctrine and belief is particularity, enfleshment, illustration. Thus

> Doctrine and life, colors and light, in one
>   When they combine and mingle, bring
> A strong regard and awe: but speech alone
>   Doth vanish like a flaring thing,
>   And in the ear, not conscience ring.
>   (from "The Temple")

It is not for nothing that most stained glass windows themselves are full of faces, brimming with story, inviting us to enter and know these experiences of faith, these truths made flesh in past time and place.

Like windows yet in my mind, images of friends within pages, seared in my memory, present in this moment, say to me still, "Come along...."

LOOKING AT FRIENDSHIP

1. What "friends within pages" have most influenced you through the years? What qualities do they embody, and how do you relate to these attributes in your life?

   Sometimes we need to see a particular face in order to grasp a concept. Christ wrote, "Greater love has no one than this, that he lays down his life for his friends." And this is exactly what he did, in his own time, in an action still touching us, his latter-day friends.

2. How can my own experience of friendship, of living with integrity among others, be enhanced by reading, with an openness to both immediate, and later, more complex responses to what I absorb?

Friendship and Maturity

I have just discovered another friend within pages, novelist Elizabeth Goudge, whose book *The Scent of Water* was recommended to me by my spiritual director. Goudge's novels, dating back to 1936, had come to my attention before, and all the characters she has created through the years, which I am discovering with delight, were there waiting within her stories. But for some reason these gifts are opened to us—or we choose to take them in hand—at different points in our life.

The following conversation in *The Scent of Water* is a wise commentary on friendship and maturity, or what we wish we had known from the beginning. Mary Lindsay, having just received a house in the English countryside as the legacy of her late aunt and namesake, has moved to the village to settle into an early retirement. She made the decision to leave London and take up quite a new kind of life for reasons she is yet beginning to understand.

In the following conversation, she discusses with a blind man, a poet whom she has just met, the prospects for friendship around her.

"'There are people here you'll like,' he said. 'Miss Anderson, one of the three bravest people I know. The other two are Colonel and Mrs. Adams. When they turn up, love them, please.'

"'How do you know I am capable of love?' she asked as they walked toward her car. 'Steady affection perhaps.'

"'If by steady you mean faithful, there you have it; the kernel of love. I imagine men long for God because of that unchanging faithfulness. The rock under the quicksands. The Psalms are full of it.'...

"'You are very direct. You haven't wasted time talking about the weather.'

"'Did you want me to?'

"'No, but most people have sufficient caution to hover on the brink a bit before they take a header into friendship.'

"'The sighted do. The blind don't have to. One of the advantages of having been blind for a good many years is that you know almost at once what people are like, and if you're going to get on. Physical appearance, and trying to use it as a relief map to show you the lay of the land, can be distracting. Without the map intuition comes alive. But blindness has its disadvantages and one of them is that you don't know the time. Should you say I am going to be late for lunch?"....

Maturing in friendship means learning to see beyond appearances, or rather, as this character illustrates, becoming able to see the face within, the true person with whom we desire to connect, the potential for friendship, for love. The second step, beyond this kind of "seeing," is the boldness of offered friendship, the leap of faith, the risk of acting on one's intuition about another that establishes the fiery cord of connection. And, of course, the other must accept in kind.

As in any story, we do not know what will happen next. And so choosing to love and extend friendship to one who appears in our path and becomes part of our "way," often in a more mysterious fashion than we can explain, carries with it great risk. And the deeper and firmer the connection, the more we may be called not only to rejoice with another through the journey ahead, but also to suffer with that person's misfortunes.

Aristotle said that "friends are more indispensable in bad fortune," but that "it is nobler to have friends in good fortune." How blessed it is to have a friend who has been with you, by you, and on your side through cycles of both fortunes.

In friendships that have lasted years, decades, there is opportunity not only to see each other through misfortunes, but also to be available to one another under many different, changing circumstances. I think of my friend Marlene in this context, now that our friendship has spanned two decades. Through many other losses, wavering friendships, disappointments in career, and rocky roads through all sorts of ventures, Marlene has been there. Hers is often the practical, incisive voice that helps me cut through to realities I'd rather not face. And she has been there also for the victories, the upturns of fate and ensuing celebration. She is a friend for all these seasons.

Her way of friendship is that of remembrance. She writes to me now that we are states apart and sends postcards to my children as she travels around the country. When a padded brown envelope arrives at the door, it is often a book she wants me to read and enjoy too.

Above all, Marlene is honest with me about what she thinks. I don't remember us wasting much time on the weather, early on in our acquaintance, when we both made the leap to "take a header into friendship." Hers is a seeing that goes beyond appearances, and she shows me how friend can complement friend. In many ways, she keeps me from blindness in areas where I need her insight. I sometimes tend to soften the harshness of facts, downgrade crises, deflect some of life's difficult realities, as I turn back quickly to things I can affirm.

Marlene has no such squeamishness. She has a gift for diagnosis that is precise, and it usually accompanies a much more gut-level suggestion for a solution than I would prefer. She has been right countless times, and probably cringed at my hopeful naivete, or sometimes wondered at my gifts of indirection and attempts to fuse the facts prematurely into a larger reality. Her approach is a great antidote to overspiritualization, while her own Christian faith is as present and tangible as the reality she describes.

Thus friend sharpens friend. We have been, above all, personally loyal, fiercely supportive of each other's careers and personal lives, valuing each other's books and articles and the sensibilities that formed these works. Through the years, amid separations both geographical and personal, we have always, by grace, been able to continue this relationship.

Thus the road goes on, and it is impossible to imagine some friends not being there with and for you, in their own way (not always comfortably), often in conviction and offering needed balance to ourselves. A friend is one who is still there, who has chosen not to break the cords, but perhaps to create them anew, along with you, at this point of the journey. That fact alone is one that partakes of heaven.

For friendship is a matter of eternity, a taste of the timelessness that we can only imagine as our destiny and a unity beyond what any of us have known to this point. When it is friendship in Christ, there is that dimension of concern for the spiritual good of the other and your own part in it—not in control, but in caretaking of the gift between you.

In this context I think also of my friend Karen, of her gentle and wise spirit, and her friendship freely given. Since her work on several mission fields has taken her literally around the world, our friendship has been measured not only in her furloughs and returns for study in the States, but in airmail letters stamped with colorful scenes and faces from the countries—Swaziland and the Republic of China—in which she has served.

In our correspondence (she is a writer, too) friendship has not only survived the distances and differences, but also grown to make us who we are when we meet more richly in person again. As she and her husband prepare now to spend a year in Portugal in language study for their new assignment in Mozambique, the ties lengthen and stretch, but I cannot imagine them ever broken.

There are two strands to friendship that I have observed over the years, and when they work together complementarily, the friendships are the strongest, like double cords that bind.

The Apostle Paul admonishes the Colossians: "Clothe yourselves with compassion, kindness, humility, gentleness and patience. Bear with each other...And over all these virtues put on love, which binds them all together in perfect unity" (Col. 3:12-14, NIV).

Bearing with one another relies first on the simple fact of having discovered each other. For Marlene and me, it was through mutual work, parallel jobs in publishing that have diverged but never lost their relevance or value to each other. Karen and I met when she was a college student and I was already an editor. I had been with her no more than twice before realizing we would be friends. Her agreement, her intuitive assent to me, little as she knew me then, made it possible.

A second strand of friendship is the uniqueness of the person as one grows to know him or her, the cords of familiarity and strength through the years of change and happenings in both lives. Friendship both happens to us and is perpetuated by us. Once when Marlene and I worked at the same company, we used to have lunch together every day, and I'm sure I started to take it for granted that I would never have to face eating alone. Having her there, day to day, became a comfortable habit that it is easy to indulge without much thought or gratitude. It was typical of our relationship that she was the first to realize our conversation was getting a little stale, that we were quick to jump on each other about petty things—a result of too much closeness.

Friendship taken for granted becomes a crutch that can keep us from growing, from having to remain fresh and genuinely interesting to the other. As a remedy (because we knew we valued what we had, and could have again), we drew apart for awhile, asked others to join us for lunch, or went separate ways some days. It was Marlene's good practical wisdom that got us through that rough spot, as well as my slowness to take offense (not always a virtue) that I could agree and go on. We both chose to let go, only to find our friendship stronger than ever when we picked it up farther down the way.

No one is there for us all the time—not even a mate in a marriage of reasonable equality—to comfort and give us the self-assurance that we need within ourselves. Each of us, to be a friend, needs a strong and lasting sense of self first, the ability to be alone, and when necessary to act alone, no matter how surrounded we are by others. It is a misconception of love—and of friendship—that it will compensate for every failure and hurt, be a consolation prize, a proof of our worth, or of anything at all that is not apparent in us as we stand alone. Instead, the person who is faithful in any relationship, is the one who dares to know us as we are and chooses to accept our humanity, the good and the bad together, for better or worse.

This willingness to walk over the long haul with another is more rare and priceless than it appears. It becomes evident on closer examination of "friendships" that many people who seem to be together are simply locked in mutual need, and perhaps even neurosis, rather than unconditional love. And love is always a continuum—no perfect relationships ever having existed.

The word for the later steps of the journey, for friendship in maturity, is always gratitude—thankfulness to be alive in the land of the living, to have companions on the way, through whatever experiences. All of life is a gift, and friendship is one we may still count as ours, if we have held lightly but firmly to its cords of flame through the years. As we are assured in the anonymous reflection, "Desiderata," no doubt the universe is unfolding as it should, despite our own actions and doubts, fears and uncertainties. And when we cannot see it, we are indeed blessed if there is another close by to remind us until we have sight again.

As I grow into what I hope eventually to call the second half of my life, I find that I am kinder to those people who share my failings (and, correspondingly, kinder to myself). I have less need to find in my friends the qualities that I lack, or attach myself to them in the hope that the connection will bring me such gifts too. We have truly learned from our friends—and valued them in the right way—when we are able to incorporate their strengths into our lives in our own way, our own style.

Later in life, our own *being* in the world, our experiences and accomplishments, often serve to healthily overshadow our *need* to have others around us. And then friendship happens more easily, less frantically, as a natural synchronicity of meeting and perceiving affinity with another.

At this stage of my life, I am not consciously seeking any one kind of friend, in the little time I have to devote to more companionship, fitted in around other duties. Yet people do come into my path, and I find myself in theirs—such as Kit, a young woman who reminds me of myself about twenty years ago, with her serious intent to write and edit. But she has made different choices than I did at that stage of life. Having interrupted her education with motherhood, she is just starting to resume her dream.

Although I didn't do it that way and had my career first, holding onto strands of it tenaciously through early motherhood, I see her as a sister. I realize how hard it is, either way, to embrace two vocations you value intensely. Her struggles are different, yet sometimes I see in her how hard it is. Holding onto a dream means sometimes being stretched almost to the thinness of pounded metal. Yet in me the dream survived—and as a survivor I can identify with and encourage her. A twenty-year difference is not so much at this stage of the road of friendship. The years up to now have been at once a life, and a blink of an eyelash.

I have learned that we must hold onto friends lightly, as they are never our possessions. Our wills are often fragile strands, and friendship can be broken—even denied, as though to re-write history—sadly, by either party. In some cases, I can only speculate as to why the other person is no longer there and try to let go.

My vocation of writing does necessitate a kind of separate-ness from others in my day-to-day work. Yet friendship is an ex-perience of life without which I cannot imagine being who I am. Any life has its solitary aspects, even in the midst of family and loved ones. Finding the mix of aloneness and community is different for each of us. For me, the commitment to vocation has been a narrowing down that, paradoxically, has led me into a much wider world of faces and voices, of possibilities and con-nections than I could ever have imagined in my early days of longing to be a writer.

The concentration on developing oneself, through relation-ships and through work, is also the context for our own trans-formation, for the breaking and remaking that constitutes life in Christ. It is only as ourselves, redeemed for service in the king-dom, that we can fully enter the world of other people, finding our place in the house, as polished stone, one among many.

From what I have seen of the journey so far, the only choice for me is more of the same—more of friendship as I have known it thus far, and in the surprising ways it may yet come to me.

Rediscovering an old friend, or making a new one who *seems* to have been one much longer, is like returning to books we have loved and rediscovering them, while adding new titles to our shelves.

Thus is friendship one way of looking at life, its progress and setbacks, gains and losses. These are my reflections of some faces of friendship in my life and what they have meant to me.

"Now I know in part; then I shall know fully, even as I am known" (1 Cor. 13:12). To know and to love are so closely con-nected in this passage. It is a knowing that is meant to go bey-ond appearances, beyond distractions that may have beset us earlier on our journey.

How could it be otherwise? We have not come to this point for nothing; we have been called to be part of those others' sto-ries, as they have been within ours. As we stay together, with, by, and for each other, we are saying, "Keep on, there is more ahead!"

"Now we see but a poor reflection as in a mirror; then we shall see face to face...."

List of Sources

Introduction

Aelred of Rievaulx, *Spiritual Friendship* (Kalamazoo, MI: Cistercian Publications), 1977.

G. Peter Fleck, *The Blessings of Imperfection* (Boston: Beacon Press), 1988.

Garrison Keillor, *Lake Wobegon News* (New York: The American Humor Institute), April 15, 1989.

Madeleine L'Engle, *The Irrational Season* (New York: The Seabury Press), 1977.

Ruth Harms Calkin, "The Garden," *Lord, I Keep Running Back to You* (Wheaton, IL: Tyndale House Publishers), 1979.

Elizabeth S. Selden, *The Book of Friendship* (Boston: Houghton Mifflin), 1947.

C. S. Lewis, *The Weight of Glory* (New York: Macmillan), 1981.

Frederick Buechner, *Now and Then* (San Francisco: Harper & Row), 1983.

Chapter One

Aelred of Rievaulx, *Spiritual Friendship*

Robert Farrar Capon, *The Third Peacock* (New York: Doubleday), 1971.

Frederick Buechner, *The Magnificent Defeat* (New York: The Seabury Press), 1966.

Bede Griffiths, *The Golden String* (Springfield, IL: Templegate), 1954, 1980.

Annie Dillard, *Holy the Firm* (New York: Harper & Row), 1977.

Herbert O'Driscoll, *A Doorway in Time* (San Francisco: Harper & Row), 1985.

Henri Nouwen, *The Living Reminder* (San Francisco: Harper & Row), 1981.

Chapter Two

Lewis Smedes, *Caring and Commitment* (San Francisco: Harper & Row), 1988.

Janna Malamud Smith, "Where Does a Writer's Family Draw the Line?" (New York: *New York Times Book Review*), November 5, 1989.

Owen Barfield, *Saving the Appearances* (New York: Harcourt Brace Jovanovich, Inc.), n.d.

Amy Carmichael, *His Thoughts Said...His Father Said...* (Fort Washington, PA: Christian Literature Crusade), 1941.

Chapter Three

e. e. cummings, "love is a place," from *No Thanks* (Liveright Publ. Corporation), 1935, 1968.

Hugh Prather, quoted in Karen Casey, *The Love Book* (Minneapolis: Winston Press), 1985.

Polly Berrien Berends, *Whole Child/Whole Parent* (New York: Harper & Row), 1983.

Amy Carmichael, *His Thoughts Said...His Father Said...*

Margaret Fuller, quoted in *The Love Book*.

Chapter Four

Anne Morrow Lindbergh, *The Unicorn and Other Poems* (New York: Vintage Books), 1972.

Aelred of Rievaulx, *Spiritual Friendship*

C. S. Lewis, *The Voyage of the Dawn Treader* (London: Geoffrey Bles), 1952.

Louisa May Alcott, *Little Women* (New York: Macmillan Publishing Co.), 1962.

Thomas Merton, *New Seeds of Contemplation* (New York: New Directions), 1961.

Harry Emerson Fosdick, quoted in *Letting God*, by A. Phillip Parham (San Francisco: Harper & Row), 1987.

Maria Harris, *Dance of the Spirit* (New York: Bantam Books), 1989.

John S. Dunne, *The Reasons of the Heart* (Notre Dame: Univ. of Notre Dame Press), 1978.

Vincent P. Collins, "Acceptance," (St. Meinrad, IN: Abbey Press), 1960.

Chapter Five

D. Bruce Lockerbie, *The Timeless Moment* (Westchester, IL: Cornerstone Books), 1980.

C. S. Lewis, *The Four Loves* (New York: Harcourt Brace Jovanovich, Inc.), 1960.

Anthony Storr, *Solitude* (New York: The Free Press), 1968.

Francis Bacon, "Of Friendship," in *Essays, Advancement of Learning, and Other Pieces* (New York: Odyssey), 1937.

George MacDonald, *The Gifts of the Child Christ* (Grand Rapids: Eerdmans), 1973.

Dorothy L. Sayers, *The Mind of the Maker* (Westport, CT: Greenwood Press), 1941.

Chapter Six

Springs of Friendship (London: Search Press, Ltd.), n.d.

C. S. Lewis, *The Great Divorce* (New York: Macmillan Publishing Co.), 1946.

Isabel Anders, *Awaiting the Child* (Cambridge, MA: Cowley Publications), 1987.

John Donne, *Devotions* (Ann Arbor: Univ. of Michigan Press), 1959.

Elizabeth S. Selden, *The Book of Friendship.*

Kahlil Gibran, *The Prophet* (New York: Alfred A. Knopf), 1964.

Chapter Seven

Urban T. Holmes, *Spirituality for Ministry* (San Francisco: Harper & Row), 1982.

Iris Murdoch, *Nuns and Soldiers* (New York: The Viking Press), 1980.

Madeleine L'Engle, *Two-Part Invention* (New York: Farrar, Straus & Giroux), 1988.

C. S. Lewis, *The Four Loves.*

Madeleine L'Engle, *The Irrational Season.*

Diogenes Allen, *Love* (Cambridge, MA: Cowley Publications), 1987.

Charles Williams, *Descent into Hell* (New York: Pellegrini & Cudahy), 1949.

John A. Sanford, *The Invisible Partners* (New York: Paulist Press), 1980.

Roy M. Gasnick, O.F.M., editor, *The Francis Book* (New York: Macmillan), 1980.

Robertson Davies, *The Manticore* (New York: The Viking Press), 1972.

Charles Williams, *The Figure of Beatrice* (London: Faber and Faber), 1943.

Chapter Eight

G. K. Chesterton quoted in Kathryn Lindskoog, *Around the Year with C. S. Lewis & His Friends* (Norwalk, CT: C. R. Gibson), 1986.

Aelred of Rievaulx, *Spiritual Friendship.*

Polly Berrien Berends, *Whole Child/Whole Parent*.

Chapter Nine

The Book of Common Prayer, The Psalter (New York: The Church Hymnal Corporation and The Seabury Press), 1977.

Ronald A. Sharp, *Friendship and Literature* (Durham, NC: Duke University Press), 1986.

Coventry Patmore, *The Rod, the Root and the Flower* (New York: Books for Libraries Press), 1950.

Charles Williams, *The Figure of Beatrice* (London: Faber and Faber), 1943.

Chapter Ten

George MacDonald quoted in Lindskoog, *Around the Year with C. S. Lewis and His Friends*.

Maria Harris, *Dance of the Spirit*.

Madeleine L'Engle, *A Wrinkle in Time* (New York: Farrar, Straus and Giroux), 1962.

Isabel Anders, *Awaiting the Child*.

Dorothy L. Sayers, *The Mind of the Maker*, Introduction by Madeleine L'Engle (San Francisco: Harper & Row), 1941, 1987.

Practical Christianity (Wheaton, IL: Tyndale House Publishers), 1987.

Chapter Eleven

Maria Harris, *Dance of the Spirit*.

Kenneth Leech, *Soul Friend* (London: Sheldon Press), 1977.

C. S. Lewis, *That Hideous Strength* (London: The Bodley Head), 1945.

George Herbert, *The Country Parson, The Temple*.

James B. Nelson, *The Intimate Connection* (Philadelphia: The Westminster Press), 1988.

Susan Howatch, *Glittering Images* (New York: Alfred A. Knopf), 1987.

William Cowper, *Olney Hymns*, quoted in Charles Williams, *The New Christian Year* (London: Oxford University Press), 1941.

Walter Wangerin, Jr., "Keepsake," in *A Miniature Cathedral and Other Poems* (San Francisco: Harper & Row), 1987.

Jonathan Raban, *For Love and Money: A Writing Life* (New York: Burlingame Books, Harper & Row), 1989.

Jacques Barzun, *Begin Here: The Forgotten Conditions of Teaching and Learning* (Chicago: University of Chicago Press), 1991.

C. S. Lewis, *Surprised by Joy* (London: Geoffrey Bles), 1956.

Walker Percy, *The Message in the Bottle* (New York: Farrar, Straus and Giroux), 1954.

Amy Carmichael, *His Thoughts Said...His Father Said...*

Margaret Cropper, *Evelyn Underhill* (London: Longmans, Green & Co.), 1958.

George Herbert, *The Country Parson, The Temple.*

Epilogue

Elizabeth Goudge, *The Scent of Water* (New York: Coward-McCann, Inc.), 1963.

COWLEY PUBLICATIONS IS A MINISTRY of the Society of St. John the Evangelist, a religious community for men in the Episcopal Church. Emerging from the Society's tradition of prayer, theological reflection, and diversity of mission, the press is centered in the rich heritage of the Anglican Communion.

Cowley Publications seeks to provide books, audio cassettes, and other resources for the ongoing theological exploration and spiritual development of the Episcopal Church and others in the body of Christ. To this end, it is dedicated to developing a new generation of theological writers, encouraging them to produce timely, creative, and stimulating publications of excellence, and making these publications available widely, reaching both clergy and lay persons.